BIRDS
OF
MORECAMBE
BAY

Grey heron - Leighton Moss

BIRDS
OF
MORECAMBE
BAY

John Wilson

Photographs by Jonathan Wilson

CICERONE PRESS
MILNTHORPE, CUMBRIA

First published 1988
ISBN 1 85284 000 5

CONTENTS

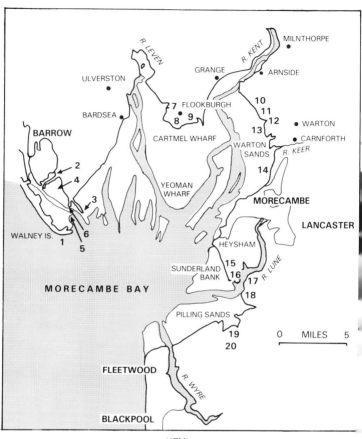

KEY

1. South Walney Nature Reserve & Bird Observatory
2. Cavendish Dock
3. Foulney Island
4. Roosecote Sands
5. Piel Island
6. Roa Island
7. Sandgate Marsh
8. West Plain Marsh
9. East Plain or Out Marsh
10. Silverdale Salt Marsh
11. Woodwell
12. Leighton Moss RSPB Reserve
13. Carnforth Salt Marshes
14. Hest Bank Salt Marsh
15. Middleton Salt Marsh
16. Sunderland Point
17. Conder Green and Glasson Dock
18. Cockersands Point
19. Pilling and Cockerham Marshes
20. Pilling and Cockerham Goose Fields

CHAPTER 1
Introduction to the Bay

Morecambe Bay is home for much of the year to one of the largest concentrations of birds to be found anywhere in Europe. Tens of thousands of birds - wildfowl, gulls, terns, cormorants and many other groups are drawn by the abundance of readily available food and by the safe resting and nesting sites provided by the Bay's sheltered shores and islands.

This book describes when, where and how many, usually occur in the intertidal area and also those which breed or visit the immediate coastal strip; an area which really forms one ecological unit.

A brief description of the Bay and the surrounding area will help to set this large concentration of birds in context. Morecambe Bay lies in the angle formed by the coastlines of south Cumbria and north Lancashire. It is a complex of five major rivers (Wyre, Lune, Keer, Kent and Leven) which flow from the Lakeland and Pennine Hills. The main outlines were moulded during the glacial period but the vast intertidal flats, which are such a feature of the Bay, have been built mainly by sand brought in by tidal action and also by river-borne silt from the land.

The most striking feature of Morecambe Bay is its size. Between the mouth of the Bay (bordered by Fleetwood on the south and Walney Island to the north) and the coastline, is an area of 507 square kilometres (195 square miles). At extreme low water, 310 square kilometres (120 square miles) of sand and mud are exposed; it is the largest continuous intertidal area in Britain.

The bed of the Bay is mainly sand mixed with some silt. Only a few limited areas such as the Lune between Lancaster and almost down to Sutherland Point can be described as muddy. Much of the sand is surprisingly firm, a fact exploited by local fishermen who drive their tractors over many areas. But where the channels are changing, quicksand is often formed.

There are few outcrops - stony areas known locally as Scars or Skeers

-which are either the remains of rocky headlands or possibly in some cases glacial deposits. Outcrops well down the tidal slope form the basis for extensive mussel beds.

Besides being cut by the five main river channels the sands are dissected by numerous gullies and creeks which drain them at low water. The central rib of the Bay is an expanse of sand known as Cartmel Wharf and Yeoman Bank from which the tide ebbs on spring tides for up to seven miles. All the larger sandbanks have been named, probably by generations of local fishermen who, like their present day successors, fished the Bay for shrimps, flatfish and shellfish. Some of these sandbank names relate to adjoining villages such as Warton and Pilling Sands. The origins of others, such as Bernard Wharf and Mort Bank, are obscure.

On the east and north of the Bay, the sandflats are bordered by extensive areas of salt marsh, which are only covered by the highest tides. These marshes are continually changing as sand is being deposited or eroded by the changing channels. A few years ago many were accreting but in recent years those on the east side have been rapidly eroded by the migrating of the Kent channel close inshore. A recent plant colonist, Cord Grass, *Spartina Townsend* has established itself on the outer edges of some salt marshes, noticeably on muddy substrates such as those off Sunderland Point and Condor Green, extending the zone of plant growth considerably in these areas. Almost all of the salt marshes are heavily grazed, mainly by sheep. Commercial turf-cutting - for lawns and bowling greens - is actively pursued on the larger marshes. Few places have extensive areas of long grass.

In contrast with the rest of the Bay the shoreline from Plumpton to Walney is mainly shingle, with quite narrow quickly shelving beaches backing onto farmland.

The islands of the Bay have a character all of their own although, strictly speaking, they are only islands at high tide, access being possible at low tide if one knows the channels. Walney, the largest of these islands, is the most important for birds, although only the southern half is considered to be part of Morecambe Bay. Much of the island is farmed, but the sand dunes, gravel pits and shingle areas at the southern end are managed as a nature reserve by the Cumbria Naturalists' Trust.

The other four islands are small and grass-covered with some brambles and scrub, especially on Chapel Island. The narrow beaches are of shingle which shelves steeply. Piel Island, with its ruined castle, is a well known landmark. A row of cottages on the island is only occupied in the summer, but the Ship Inn is staffed by a licensee and his family, and there is a ferry service in summer from Roa Island (which is not a real island at all!). Chapel Island takes its name from the chapel (now ruined) which was built on the limestone outcrop in the mouth of the River Leven. Both these island buildings are legacies from the monks of Furness Abbey.

Although the Bay is attractively set against the backdrop of the Lakeland hills to the north and the Pennines to the east, much of the coastal strip is flat or undulating except for the wooded limestone outcrops of Whitbarrow Scar, Arnside Knott and Warton Crag. Limestone woodland is also a feature of the east side of the Leven, round Grange-over-sands and the Arnside/Silverdale area. Large areas of the coastal strip are devoted to agriculture, mainly stock farming, with only small areas of arable land - at least in recent years. Open water areas include the man-made reservoir of Cavendish Dock at Barrow-in-Furness, while Urswick Tarn provides a focal point for water birds. The R.S.P.B. Reserve at Leighton Moss near Silverdale, with its extensive areas of reed beds, scrub and shallow open water, provides a unique fenland habitat. The industrial and residential towns of Fleetwood, Morecambe and Barrow-in-Furness, along with many small towns and villages completes this brief description of the coastal strip. The area is covered by Ordnance Survey 1:50,000 sheets Nos. 96, 97 and 102.

Morecambe Bay weather is generally mild with a preponderance of westerly winds. Snow or ice rarely remains long because of the warming effect of the sea and tides. Ice forms on the intertidal area only during the severest of spells.

The life blood of an estuary is the tide which, twice daily, covers the sand with nutrient-rich water, shaping the lives of all its inhabitants. An understanding of the tidal cycle is therefore essential to any study of the birds of an estuary. Tides occur at approximately 12 hour intervals, and advance roughly one hour each day. There is a week of low tides (neap tides) followed by a week of high tides (spring tides). Overlying this fortnightly tidal rhythm is an annual rhythm, by which the spring tides become progressively higher towards the vernal and autumnal equinoxes. The tide ebbs further on a spring than on a neap tide, so the largest areas are exposed during the periods of spring tides. The difference in height between the levels of the lowest and highest tides is up to 3.5 metres (10 feet).

Tide tables, published for at least four areas in the Bay, differ in the predictions of height because of the different sites where the tide is measured. All tide heights referred to in this guide are based on Liverpool predictions, as these are most readily available locally. Tide times given in the Liverpool tables are generally correct for the Morecambe area, but high tide on the west and north of the Bay is usually about 15 minutes later than these. Tidal predictions are printed in all the local papers. Tide tables can be purchased from stationary or fishing tackle shops in the area.

A WORD OF WARNING: It is essential to consult the tide tables before venturing onto the Bay. Tidal heights can be affected by strong winds, especially from the west, Under such conditions increases of up to a metre are not uncommon. Conversely, calm anticyclone conditions can result in lower tides than predicted.

Best bird watching opportunities occur in the spring tides as the birds are concentrated close inshore or on the salt marshes or shingle beaches. It is best under such conditions to arrive one or two hours before high tide and watch the arrival of birds as they are displaced from their feeding areas by the incoming tide. Always keep to the edges of the salt marshes as these can be very dangerous with an incoming tide. Show consideration both to the birds and other bird-watchers by not disturbing the birds by too close an approach. Binoculars are essential and a telescope desirable. Full details of the best birdwatching sites are given in Chapter 5.

Wildfowling is widely practised but is strictly controlled by the local Wildfowlers' Associations. Dawn and dusk shooting are most popular. The shooting season below high water mark extends from September 1st to February 21st but ends on January 31st above high water mark. Three large 'no shooting' areas have been established to protect roosting wildfowl from disturbance. The Wyre-Lune Sanctuary is a National Wildfowl Refuge and covers almost all the inter-tidal area on the south bank of the Lune. The R.S.P.B. Morecambe Bay Reserve extends from Hest Bank almost to Blackstone Point near Arnside and protects 6100 acres. The South Walney Reserve is also the centre of a large no-shooting area.

For many years the serious study of birds of Morecambe Bay was restricted to the more favoured and easily accessible areas, with no co-ordination between observers. However, the publication in 1976 of a desk study into the possibility of building a Morecambe Bay barrage stimulated intensive research. In an attempt to assess the implications of this far-reaching scheme, the Nature Conservancy Council, the R.S.P.B., local Naturalists' Trusts and the Wildfowlers' Associations cooperatively studied the numbers, distributions, migrations and feeding ecology of waders and wildfowl. This scheme was quickly extended to all other British estuaries and became the British Trust for Ornithology's Estuaries Enquiry which has continued up to the present time. This research has formed the basis of much of the material in the succeeding chapters.

This everchanging world of water and sand has provided me with some of my most thrilling and fascinating bird watching, I hope I can help readers to share some of these experiences.

CHAPTER 2
Waders and Wildfowl

These are the most important groups of birds occuring on the Bay. The B.T.O. Estuaries Enquiry has shown Morecambe Bay to be the most important estuary for waders in Britain. While not as important for wildfowl, the Bay does hold some significant populations. This chapter describes in detail all the species that *regularly* occur within the Bay, *irregular* species are also included but with less detail.

WADERS

To watch wading birds successfully on an estuary one needs to understand something of their feeding and roosting behaviour. This is dealt with in greater detail in Chapter 5 but a brief introduction is given here. Most waders are restricted to the intertidal area for feeding; they spread out at low water over the sandflats to exploit the rich feeding grounds. As the tide comes in they are forced to retreat for although they can swim for brief periods they prefer not to. During the high tide period they generally cease to feed, resting or 'roosting'.

The Oystercatcher, for example, feed a great deal on mussels which occur only on the lower shore and are often covered 2-3 hours before high tide. The birds cease feeding and start to assemble first of all in sub-roosts on the still exposed sand banks then moving quickly to the final roost site. By contrast, Dunlin feed on small sandhoppers and marine snails which occur right up to the shore. This means they can continue feeding almost until the last areas of sand are covered.

This time difference means there is usually an orderly arrival at the roost site, with the species which feed lower down the tidal cycle (mainly the larger waders) arriving first and the upper shore feeders (mainly the smaller birds) arriving last. Birds also leave the roost in the same order with the lower shore birds leaving last, often 2-3 hours after high tide. On neap tides the birds roost on the still exposed sand banks but on spring tides they resort to the shingle beaches and salt marshes. When these are covered by extreme high or wind blown tides

*Oystercatcher -
Jenny Brown's
Point*

13

they usually move onto fields a little way inland.

This assembling at the roost gives wader watching an interesting further dimension. In some areas the best watching can be had by positioning oneself on the flight line to the roost some 2-2½ hours before high tide. At other sites this is impossible (and would be dangerous) so the hour or so around high tide is best.

In the following species accounts the figures for population levels are taken from the Estuaries Enquiry data and usually refer to average figures.

OYSTERCATCHER
Commonest of the larger waders, the oystercatcher occurs in large flocks in all areas of the Bay. The black and white plumage and orange bill are distinctive. Flocks are noisy, keeping up a constant piping especially on the feeding grounds. The total wintering population in recent years has been between 30-40,000 with a peak of 45-50,000 during the autumn passage from August to October. Oystercatchers feed on the extensive mussel beds, especially those at Rampside, Heysham and Knott End. In mild winter weather, especially when the fields are wet, many move inland to feed on earthworms. This habit of feeding in the fields started during the 1962/63 winter when severe cold weather killed off most of the cockles, a favoured food. Over the last few years there has been a decline in the numbers feeding in this habitat, possibly because there has been something of a resurgence of the cockle population. All the wader roosts around the Bay have their share of Oystercatchers, but the largest numbers are to be found in the Foulney - Piel - Walney complex, with up to 20,000 birds being frequently recorded.

It breeds on shingle beaches and salt marshes around the Bay with a total population on the coast of around 250 pairs.

AVOCET
There are four records of this attractive vagrant during the last twenty years, two each in spring and autumn.

LITTLE RINGED PLOVER
A recent and increasing colonist. Up to four pairs have bred recently on the edge of a large salt marsh. Birds usually arrive in early April and depart in September. Most records, usually of single birds or family groups, are from salt marsh pools or inland waters.

RINGED PLOVER
The dainty ringed plover is readily recognised in both winter and

summer plumage by its brown upperparts and white underparts, with a contrasting black and white ringed pattern round the neck and head. The 'run, stop and dip' feeding action distinguishes the ringed plover from the same sized dunlin, even at long range.

Pairs nest on almost all the shingle beaches and on some of the larger well-grazed salt marshes. The total population is about 75 pairs. This species is uncommon in winter, usually only 2-300 occurring, mainly on the shingle beaches of the Morecambe area and the west of the Bay from Walney to the Ulverston area. However, large numbers pass through the Bay in spring and late summer. Peak numbers occur in May when up to 7000 have been recorded, smaller numbers occur in August and September with usually *c.* 2500 at peak passage. During migration periods numbers are well distributed throughout the Bay.

DOTTEREL
A rare passage migrant not recorded every year. Occasional records of small 'trips' of usually under five birds in May, almost always at this time on coastal fields. On autumn passage it is even rarer, with usually just single birds at times on the salt marshes.

GOLDEN PLOVER
The golden plover's winter plumage is golden brown on the upper parts with lighter underparts that become black when in summer plumage. This field feeding species regularly mixes with lapwing.

Large flocks feed around the Bay, usually on low lying fields which are traditional sites regularly used each year while other apparently suitable fields are ignored. Such favoured sites include the fields round Cockersands Abbey, Heysham Moss, Bolton-le-Sands, the airfield near Flookburgh and on South Walney.

The intertidal area is only resorted to during severe cold spells, but large numbers use the mussel beds and stoney scars as a nocturnal roost.

GREY PLOVER
One of the most attractive waders, the grey plover, has a silver-grey winter plumage with a noticeable black patch under the wings. When in summer plumage it is especially striking, a silver grey back spangled with black underparts.

Only small numbers occur on the Bay, because this species prefers muddy substrates. The population has increased somewhat in recent years and peak counts can now approach 500 birds, - almost double the figure of ten years ago. Largest numbers usually occur during the passage periods. The Lune is a preferred area and roosting flocks can

Knot - Hest Bank

be seen on the Middleton roost and around Fluke Hall near Pilling. Two other favoured areas are the shingle beach along Rampside and the outer shore of Walney.

LAPWING
This familiar wader, with its black and white plumage, long thin crest and broad rounded wings, is abundant throughout the area. Large flocks occur in the low-lying fields around the Bay and at times on the sandbanks of the upper estuaries and on the salt marshes, areas regularly used during spring and autumn passage and frosty weather. If the weather becomes very severe, however, almost all the population leaves, probably moving to Ireland.

Numbers breed on the salt marshes and wet fields all around the Bay.

KNOT
This is one of the commonest waders and provides one of the greatest spectacles, not only by its large numbers, but when massed flocks twist and turn in unison, showing first the dark upperparts then the light underparts. The effect is of a distant cloud of smoke. In winter the knot is grey with lighter underparts. Its stocky build and larger size differentiate it from dunlin with which it often associates. From

late April onwards, the summer plumage of red underparts and dark upper parts is donned and birds occur in such plumage until mid-September.

The wintering population is large, with 70-80,000, although numbers have been lower over the last few years, - a decline probably caused by a series of poor breeding seasons in the high arctic. The Morecambe area, with the roost at Hest Bank, normally holds the largest population and the species is always well represented on both banks of the Lune. The Walney area is important during cold spells, at which time marked movements occur within the Bay, some birds leaving, probably to Ireland.

Largest numbers usually occur in spring, when upwards of 100,000 birds may be present for a short time. Many of these are birds which have wintered further south and are heading for the Greenland breeding grounds. Before they depart they often gather together in very large flocks, Hest Bank, the Foulney area and the Lune are favoured localities. Numbers slump dramatically in May although in cold springs departure can be delayed until well into the month, only a few hundred non-breeders remain by late May. Numbers increase again in late July with the first arrivals usually seen on the Lune and much of the late summer population of up to 15,000 birds is in this area. In the 1960's and 70's the large wintering population used to arrive in mid-to-late October but in recent years the major arrival has been delayed until November or even December.

SANDERLING
In winter plumage, the sanderling is the whitest of the small waders; it has a marked dark 'shoulder' patch. In summer plumage the upperparts are rich brown with most of the underparts white. The sanderling is the most active and quick moving of the waders.

This species is uncommon in winter with no more than 100 on the Lune, often round Fluke Hall, and a similar number along the West Shore of Walney Island. Numbers start to arrive in late April but the peak of spring passage is in the last week of May and the first few days of June, during which period up to 15,000 have been recorded, almost all in full summer plumage. Return passage starts in late July and goes on throughout August and into September but peak numbers which usually occur in early August rarely exceed 2,500 birds.

LITTLE STINT
Appears in small numbers each Autumn, mostly September. Usually frequents salt marsh pools or muddy estuaries with the River Condor at Condor Green being especially favoured. Only occasional records in

Sanderling - Sunderland Point

Spring, usually in May.

TEMMINCK'S STINT
A rare vagrant, not recorded annually. Usual records are of single birds on spring or autumn passage on salt march pools or inland waters.

PECTORAL SANDPIPER
A rare vagrant with 4 sightings over the last ten years.

CURLEW SANDPIPER
An autumn passage migrant, regular in small numbers each year. A few adults are recorded each July, but the main passage is of juvenile birds between late August and early October. Usually 10-20 most years but in 'invasion' years up to 70 have been recorded at peak. Conder Green is the most favoured locality and in recent years the Allen Pool on Carnforth Marsh. Very rare in spring.

PURPLE SANDPIPER
This rather dark, yellow-legged small wader prefers rocky coasts so is scarce in the Bay. Regular in winter at two localities with up to 10 on the rocks at Red Nab at Heysham and a maximum of around 100 on the West Shore of Walney Island. Only occasional records elsewhere,

but in recent years a few have used the newly exposed breakwater at Silverdale irregularly.

DUNLIN

This the commonest of the smaller waders, is grey brown above and white below in winter but sports a black belly and bright rusty underparts in summer plumage. The species engages in similar aerial movements to those described under knot with which it often mixes.

The total wintering population is usually 40-50,000 spread generally throughout the Bay. The largest numbers (up to 20,000) roost on the Flookburgh marshes. Autumn passage starts in mid July with the arrival of many adult birds, juveniles appear in August when the autumn peak can reach up to 20,000. Numbers decline in September but increase to the wintering level by mid October. There is a marked spring passage of similar proportions in April and May but only a few summering birds are left in June.

A few pairs nest on some of the larger salt marshes.

RUFF

A regular passage migrant on the salt marshes and damp pasture. Usually under five recorded on spring passage from mid April through May. Males are often in full plumage at this time and on occasions have been seen to display. Returning birds occur from late July on to September with peak counts of up to 50 birds. Favoured localities include Condor Green the Allen Pool, Kent Estuary and South Walney. An occasional bird in mid winter.

Dunlin - Morecambe Bay

JACK SNIPE

A winter visitor that is undoubtedly under-recorded due to its skulking habit, preferring damp fields and the upper salt marshes. First arrivals are recorded in September. Leighton Moss and the flooded sections of Carnforth Marsh are favoured localities with up to 50 having been recorded on occasions, but the normal wintering population is 10-20 birds. One's and two's have been recorded at many other marshy localities. A few linger well into May.

SNIPE

This well known wader with its spangled and striped plumage and zig-zag flight breeds in many marshy fields around the Bay, although drainage of such habitats has reduced it recently.

Most marshy fields and the upper salt marshes hold numbers in winter, the largest numbers being recorded at Leighton Moss and the flooded section of Carnforth Marsh, where up to 500 have been recorded. The wintering population arrives in September, often reaching a peak in October and November. Birds move out during cold spells. Rarely seen on the open estuaries but occurs in numbers on muddy creeks especially at Condor Green.

A few pairs breed on the larger salt marshes and in wet fields on the coastal strip.

WOODCOCK

This woodland wader is locally common in the wooded areas both as a breeding bird and as a winter visitor. Peak numbers occur when cold weather further east pushes birds across to the west.

BLACK-TAILED GODWIT

A regular passage migrant in small numbers. There are many records of single birds and small groups from the open estuary, salt marsh pools and inland waters. Occasional flocks of up to 25 have been recorded, usually in late July. The Allen Pool and flooded sections of Carnforth Marsh have become regular haunts. Numbers in spring are usually lower than autumn. There are a few winter records. Best distinguished from the bar-tailed godwit by its white wing bar.

BAR-TAILED GODWIT

In winter plumage the bar-tailed godwit superficially resembles the curlew, but is smaller with a long slightly up-tilted bill. The summer plumage is striking chestnut.

This species has a surprisingly limited distribution on the Bay. Almost all the regular wintering population of *c.* 7000 occur on the

Lune. Small numbers usually 1-200 and occasionally up to 750 - occur at Hest Bank and South Walney with occasional small flocks elsewhere. Birds in summer plumage begin to arrive in late July and mainly roost on the south Lune. There is a gradual build up in numbers during August and September and the wintering population is present by October. There is usually a gradual movement from the south bank of the Lune to the Middleton roost, and by mid-winter the bulk of the birds are roosting there.

Numbers decline quickly in March and early April leaving a small summering population of *c.* 250 which are usually centered on the Kent estuary.

WHIMBREL

The whimbrel, is a smaller version of the curlew but has a distinctive striped crown and a shorter decurved bill. It also has a distinctive call- a single note rapidly repeated six or seven times.

Regular in small numbers as a spring (April/May) and autumn (July/September) passage migrant, often mixing with curlew flocks. Although well distributed during these periods, especially favoured areas are East Plain Marsh near Humphrey Head, Carnforth Marsh and Sunderland Point. Total numbers at any one time rarely exceed 50 birds.

CURLEW

This large wader is recognised by its brown streaked plumage, long decurved bill and familiar whistling call. The curlew is wary and takes to the wing at the first sign of danger. Since shooting of this species was stopped it has become more approachable. It favours the larger salt marshes as roosting sites, especially in late summer when other roosts are regularly disturbed.

Major areas are Sandgate and other upper Leven marshes, the upper Kent, Carnforth Marsh and the Lune estuary especially Colloway marsh. The locations of these roosts at or near the main river mouths may be influenced by the large numbers that regularly feed inland throughout much of the year but fly back to the Bay at dusk. Such birds not only feed in low lying fields on the coastal strip but in many of the river valley fields.

Because of this field feeding habit, total numbers are difficult to assess as many are missed on estuary roost counts. The mid-winter roosting population at high tide is normally 3-4,000 birds, but during cold weather this can double, presumably by birds unable to feed inland under such conditions. Peak numbers occur during the autumn passage (July-August) with 12-14,000 present. The spring passage

Curlew - Jenny Brown's Point

starts in late February and continues until early April, with flocks often moving inland at this time, usually calling excitedly. Total numbers at this time rarely exceed 5,000. Upwards of 2,000 remain throughout the summer, presumably immature non-breeding birds.

A few pairs breed on the larger salt marshes and in the coastal strip.

SPOTTED REDSHANK

A passage migrant in small numbers. Spring passage, usually under 5 in total, between April and mid-June. Return passage starts in late June on to September with usually slightly higher numbers than in spring. Favoured sites are Condor Green, Carnforth Marsh, Leighton Moss and the Kent and Leven estuaries. Wintering birds occur most years most regularly in the upper Leven but occasionally elsewhere.

REDSHANK
The redshank has a mainly brown plumage but with a white trailing edge to the wing, its red legs are a distinguishing feature. Redshanks are well distributed in the Bay, with the largest populations in the Walney, Meathop and Hest Bank areas. The mid-winter population is normally 5-6,000 birds. Peak numbers of up to 12,000 are reached in September and early October with passage being evident from July onwards, there is a much smaller passage in March and early April. Large numbers of redshanks often feed inland, especially when the fields are waterlogged. Some of the littoral feeders may roost in fields on even the lower spring tides.

Numbers breed on most of the salt marshes, although the increasingly intense sheep grazing on most marshes has robbed them of nesting cover and breeding number have declined in recent years. The same can be said about the field nesting populations where increased land drainage has damaged many suitable sites.

GREENSHANK
The greenshank is taller and lighter in colour than the redshank, it has green legs and in flight shows dark wings and a conspicuous white V on the lower back as it flies. It has a loud ringing distinctive call often redered *tew-tew-tew*.

It can be seen in small numbers (usually no more than 10) in spring. Larger numbers occur in autumn and the total Bay population can be around the 100 mark in August and September. Some linger well into October and a few occasionally winter, especially on the upper Leven and at South Walney. Favoured area at passage time include the upper Kent and Leven, the Allen Pool and Leighton Moss, but birds can be flushed from any salt marsh creek or pool at this time.

GREEN SANDPIPER
A passage migrant in small numbers, occasionally wintering. Spring passage from late March to May and autumn passage late June to October. Usually single birds but occasionally small groups of up to five. Salt marsh pools especially the Allen Pool are regular haunts, along with inland water - Leighton Moss being the most favoured. Single wintering birds have been recorded at the above localities and

Turnstone - Jenny Brown's Point

on the upper parts of several of the larger salt marshes; the
Flookburgh marshes being a regular haunt.

WOOD SANDPIPER
Passage migrant in very small numbers. Very few records on spring
passage; usually recorded from Leighton Moss between early May and
mid-June.

More widespread on autumn passage from late July to early
October. Favoured localities are Leighton Moss, the Allen Pool,
Conder Green and South Walney, rarely more than single birds.

COMMON SANDPIPER
This small sandpiper is brown above with light underparts. It has a
very characteristic tilted forward stance and a bobbing action. A
summer visitor to fast flowing streams and rivers it is well distributed
around the bay on both spring and autumn passage, regularly
frequenting the river estuaries, tidal creeks, salt marsh pools and
inland waters. Total numbers probably rarely exceed 150 at any one
time. Spring passage occurs from mid-April through May and
returning birds are present from early July to early October.
Occasional birds have wintered.

TURNSTONE

This specialised bird gets its name from its habit of turning over small stones in search of sandhoppers. On the Bay it feeds mainly on the mussel beds and shingle areas. The plumage in winter is a drab mixture of brown-black upperparts and white underparts, but in summer it is a rather striking mixture of black, white and rich brown. The legs are orange. The black and white pattern on the wings is very striking in flight.

The total wintering population is usually around the 1,750 mark with the majority of the population centred on the mussel beds at Knott End, Heysham and Rampside and usually roosting on the nearest shingle beach to these feeding areas. It is a very tame bird; up to 200 roost on the pier at Morecambe or on a small strip of shingle below the Morecambe promenade opposite the Broadway Hotel. Peak numbers often occur in August when over 2,000 have been counted. First arrivals are in late July. The spring passage is often noted in April with an increase on the wintering population but numbers decline rapidly in May, although in a cold spring they can linger to mid-month. A few individuals summer on the Bay.

RED-NECKED PHALAROPE

A very rare passage migrant, recorded five times in the last twenty years on autumn passage at Walney and Rossall.

GREY PHALAROPE

A storm driven autumn vagrant, not recorded annually. Occurences have been usually of solitary birds between September and December and most often after October gales. Almost all records are from the mouth of the Bay.

OTHER SPECIES

The following eight species have occurred as rare visitors during the last twenty years. The numbers of sightings for each species is also given:

stone curlew 2, collared pratincole 1, white-rumped sandpiper 1, baird's sandpiper 1, buff-breasted sandpiper 2, lesser yellowlegs 1, marsh sandpiper 1, wilson's phalarope 1.

WILDFOWL

Wildfowl, like waders, are best watched at or around high tide. This is because they often float close inshore on the flooding tide. Most species sit out the high tide period on the water, although some species, for example eiders, often haul out onto any undisturbed beach. Wigeon often graze the salt marshes at high tide. Many of the hints given for watching waders at the start of this chapter also apply to wildfowl on the intertidal areas. However, it is perhaps best to explain a little of the feeding behaviour of wildfowl because an understanding of this will enhance one's bird watching of this attractive group.

Many species of duck do much of their feeding after dark, so they are often using the intertidal area and some inland waters as day-time roosts and they flight to and from the feeding grounds at dusk and dawn. Only a few species, the eider is a good example, feed on the intertidal area. They feed, mainly on mussels at low water and on the ebb and flow tides. Geese by contrast feed inland on the fields during the day and flight back to roost on the intertidal areas at dusk. Wildfowl numbers and distribution are much more difficult to assess than waders. This is because they sit out the tide on the water and a proportion of the population can often be missed, especially on a windy day when the choppy sea makes observation difficult as flocks bob up and down on the water, or on a calm day when they are spread out of sight on the vast areas of Morecambe Bay.

Population estimates are taken from the wildfowl counts for the area which are carried out monthly from September to March. In this section Leighton Moss wildfowl are only covered briefly - they are covered in more detail in Chapter 4.

MUTE SWAN

This well-known species is easily identified by its orange and black bill and the S-shaped neck. Up to 10 pairs breed in the coastal strip with the 3-4 pairs at Leighton Moss being the largest breeding concentration. Many breeding pairs are resident except when frozen out during cold spells, or when moulting. Immature birds congregate at several sites and there is marked movement of birds, many from outside the area, to moult at Cavendish Dock, where in recent years up to 115 have assembled. Up to fifty congregate on the Lune at Lancaster for much of the year; these are mainly immature birds. This is only about a quarter of the numbers that used this area in the 60's and early 70's. Since the flooding of the upper part of Carnforth marsh around 20 birds have wintered there.

BEWICK'S SWAN

The smallest swan with a shorter neck and a small rounded patch of yellow on the bill. An irregular visitor in small numbers during autumn and winter to the salt marshes. Most regular on the Lune with signs of a small population perhaps establishing itself there in recent years. In spring or late winter in some years flocks of up to 100+ passage through, usually in early March, pausing on the estuaries or inland waters for a day or so. These are probably part of the wintering Irish population on return migration to the Russian breeding grounds.

WHOOPER SWAN
A triangular yellow base to the bill, larger size and straight neck separate this species.

Mainly a transitory winter visitor, with single birds or small groups appearing for a few days or occasionally weeks, on the salt marsh pools or inland waters. Records are spread throughout the period from October to April with most occurrences in October/November and February/March. Most of these birds are probably in transit to Martin Mere in south Lancashire where up to 100+ winter.

BEAN GOOSE
A rare winter visitor, only very occasional single birds or small groups with the pinkfeet flocks in the Pilling/Cockerham area usually in February or March.

PINK-FOOTED GOOSE
This goose has a dark head and neck, pink legs, and a black and pink bill. It is a little smaller than the grey lag.

Between 1-2,000 winter on the south bank of the Lune. They feed inland during the day, on the farmland, and roost on the sandbanks of the Lune on the Wyre/Lune Sanctuary. Numbers increase from the turn of the year and especially after the end of the inland shooting season on Jan. 31st, and up to 5-8,000 have been recorded in February and early March. Flocks are frequent in other parts of the area, either on passage or when shooting disturbance is intense on the feeding grounds. During heavy snow, flocks appear in many other areas and can remain for several weeks if grazing is available. First birds regularly arrive in September and some linger well into April.

SNOW GOOSE
Very rare vagrant, a few recorded with the pinkfeet in spring in recent years of both races. May be genuine wild birds or possibly escapes.

GREY-LAG GOOSE
This species is distinguished by its pale grey fore-wing, orange legs and bill. There is a feral breeding population of 10-15 pairs now established at Leighton Moss where the total feral population is around 70 birds, including immatures. There are indications that the feral breed-

ing population may be spreading to other areas.

This establishment of the feral breeding population has made it impossible to be sure of the origins of birds seen in winter as other feral populations are also well established in the north-west.

The winter numbers are around the 400 mark. In recent years they have been mainly centred on the upper sections of Carnforth Marsh, but flocks also visit the Kent and Lune valleys. The sandbanks around the Keer estuary and the meres at Leighton Moss are used as a night-time roost. Numbers start to increase in October, but decline and become more scattered from mid-February on.

WHITE-FRONTED GOOSE

This species can be recognised easily by a conspicuous broad white forehead and black bars on the underparts. Birds of the European race have pink bills and those of the Greenland race have orange-yellow bills.

Small numbers of both races feed with the pinkfeet in winter on the south side of the Lune. Usually under 10 birds, but up to 30 have occurred. Most sightings are in February and March. Both races occur but the European is the more usual.

CANADA GOOSE

Distinguished from other 'black geese' by brown body and white patch on cheek.

Breeds in numbers in the Lune valley and recently at Leighton Moss and small flocks occasionally wander to the salt marshes or inland waters. In some years larger flocks are seen in June and July, often moving north and these may well be on moult migration from the Lune.

BARNACLE GOOSE

The black and white plumage with a conspicuous white face identifies this species.

A regular winter visitor in small numbers, total population usually 10-20 birds. In autumn often occurs with the grey lags on Carnforth Marsh and occasionally elsewhere. From January to March small numbers usually occur with the pinkfeet at Pilling. Occasional records throughout the year of feral birds, often with other geese.

BRENT GOOSE

Smallest and darkest of the 'black geese' with a small white fleck on the side of a dark neck. Both races - the dark and light bellied forms occur.

A regular winter visitor in very small numbers; usually under five each winter. Foulney is a favoured area and small groups occur with the pinkfeet flocks in late winter in the Pilling/Cockerham area.

SHELDUCK

This large duck is easily recognised, being generally white with a chestnut breast band and green head. The sexes have similar plumage. The shelduck breeds in some numbers in all suitable areas around the Bay. It nests in rabbit holes but since myxomatosis decimated the rabbit population they have used natural holes much more, necessitating a move further inland. Young birds are brought down to the estuaries as soon as they are hatched. During the breeding season large flocks of apparently non-breeding birds occur often sitting on the water in pairs - the largest numbers on the Leven estuary with up to 500 birds.

Adults migrate in late June and early July to their moulting area. Movements take place on calm evenings. The Keer estuary is one of the main departure points for the Bay population on their journey to the moulting grounds off the German coast. The return movement begins in September and the whole population is back by November.

In mid-winter the largest flocks occur at the head of the Bay with up to 3,000 birds at the peak, with the major concentration at Humphrey Head. Other concentrations of up to 1,000 birds at times occur on the Kent and the Lune and slightly smaller numbers from Hest Bank to Jenny Brown's Point. The total wintering population can reach 7,500.

WIGEON

The drake is very distinctive with a short blue bill, chestnut head with a buff crown, grey under-parts and a white area on the wing which is very conspicuous in flight. The drake has a clear whistling call.

The wigeon is the commonest wintering duck in the bay with a total population at peak from 6-9,000 birds. Concentrations of around 1,000 birds have been recorded in the Lune estuary, off Carnforth Marsh, the Flookburgh marshes, Foulney and Rampside and South Walney. Cavendish Dock used to hold up to 1,500 but in recent years has held only around 500. Upwards of 500 have recently started to use the flooded section of Carnforth Marsh.

An occasional bird or small party may summer, but the first influx takes place in late July, with large numbers usually present by mid-October. Numbers often decline in February and on through March to leave only a small passage in April.

GADWALL

The male is greyish with a contrasting black 'stern', the female is

Teal - Leighton Moss

mottled brown, both have a white wing patch.

The only regular haunt is at Leighton Moss where it has bred on occasions. The peak population of up to 45 occurs in September/October. Numbers decline to a winter population of 10-20 with usually 5-10 in spring. Occasional small numbers elsewhere especially on Carnforth Marsh when Leighton is frozen.

TEAL

Smallest of our ducks, the handsome drake is easily recognised by its chestnut head with a broad green stripe through the eye, and at a distance by a horizontal white line above the wing and a yellow patch below the tail. The sombre duck has a black and green speculum and light under-parts.

Up to five pairs nest at Leighton Moss and an occasional pair elsewhere. Small numbers of teal can be found in many areas of the Bay, especially on the larger salt marsh pools. The total wintering population is around 4-6,000. The major concentrations are at Leighton Moss and nearby flooded areas of Carnforth Marsh where up to 2,000 have been recorded. Up to 1,500 have occurred at South Walney and 500 in the upper Leven. Some start to arrive in late July but the main arrival is in October. Numbers decline in February but some numbers remain until mid-April or in a cold spring into early May.

MALLARD

This well-known species is easily recognised, the male has a dark green head, chestnut breast and a white neck ring. Both sexes have a conspicuous blue wing patch or speculum. Especially where birds are released by wildfowlers, birds with colour mixes of white, brown or black are common. Large numbers breed in the area, around 100 pairs breed in the Leighton Moss area and almost all the salt marshes have breeding pairs.

Mallard occur almost anywhere there is water, from the village pond to the open sea. The wintering population is between 5-8,000 birds. Up to 1,000 have been recorded on each side of the Lune, often sitting well off shore at high tide. Around 500 winter at Leighton Moss, but the largest numbers occur here from July to September when up to 2,500 have been counted, many of them come to the Reserve to moult, they flight out in the evenings to feed on the sand flats, flighting back in the morning. They are flightless for a short period. The Kent and Leven estuaries hold up to 500 each and similar numbers have been recorded in the Walney area. Largest numbers occur on the estuaries when inland waters are frozen.

Mallard - Leighton Moss

PINTAIL

The drake is easily recognised by its long tail, combined with a striking pattern of brown head and throat, with a white breast and stripe up the side of the neck. The duck has a more pointed tail and slender neck than other species.

Wintering numbers of this duck are highly variable. Numbers occur each year in the favoured areas but there are very marked 'pintail' years and at such times numbers also occur at several other areas, but are absent in years of low numbers. In a good year the wintering population can exceed 3,000 whereas in other years it was well under 1,000. The major pintail area is from the Flookburgh marshes round to the Kent estuary, with a peak count here of 2,300. Up to 400 have ocurred off Silverdale; these flight into Leighton Moss on occasions. The first arrivals are often noted in late July and the wintering population is usually present by mid-October. Numbers decline from February on with a few birds lingering into April and early May.

GARGENY

An occasional breeder at Leighton Moss, this summer visitor occurs annually in very small numbers from late March to early October. Almost all records are from Leighton Moss or the flooded section of Carnforth Marsh with a very occasional record from South Walney. Total population in one year rarely exceeds five birds. One wintering record from Leighton Moss.

SHOVELER

Both sexes are easy recognisable by their large bill. The drake has striking plumage of dark green head, white breast and chestnut flanks. This species is restricted as a breeding species to Leighton Moss with about 20 pairs breeding in the general area of the Moss and the flooded section of Carnforth Marsh.

Leighton holds the largest population with an autumn peak of 2-400. Numbers decline with the first frost but about 100-500 winter. Up to 50 have occurred on both the Cockerham and Sandgate marshes and irregularly off Hest Bank. Numbers decline in February although there is often a small influx into Leighton in April.

POCHARD

Male easily distinguished by dark chestnut head and neck, contrasting with the dark breast and grey body. This is normally a freshwater diving duck only appearing on the sea during severe cold spells. Up to seven pairs breed at Leighton Moss where up to 50 occur in late summer. Usually under 20 in winter with a spring peak of up to 100.

Shoveler - Leighton Moss
Pochard - Leighton Moss

Up to 600 have been recorded at Cavendish Dock in winter; largest numbers often occuring when inland waters are frozen.

TUFTED DUCK

The white panel on the sides, and marked drooping crest identify the male. The female is browner.

Up to 10 pairs breed at Leighton Moss, where only about 20-30 winter, but up to 120 occur in spring. Up to 450 have been recorded on Cavendish Dock. Here peak numbers often occur in November and December.

SCAUP

The drake is at once distinguished by its grey back and white sides, with black head, breast and tail. The duck is generally dark but with a large white patch at the base of the bill.

This species is mainly a duck of the lower estuary, although it is surprisingly scarce at Walney. The largest regular flock is off Bardsea where maximum numbers in recent years have been 100-120, although the usual number is 50-80. At high tide most birds sit between the mainland and Chapel Island and float on ebbing tide towards Bardsea. Small numbers, usually no more than 10-15, are regular off Morecambe promenade (usually off the Broadway mussel bed). Occasional birds or small groups are seen in the Lune or off Jenny Brown's Point.

The first arrivals are in late September, with most present by early November. Most have left by early April but a few may linger into May.

EIDER

The drake is unmistakable with white back and black under-parts. The head and neck are white with a black crown. Both sexes have a heavy build and a triangular-shaped head.

Eiders first colonised Walney in 1949 and the one pair in that year has increased to upwards of 950 nests, mainly on Walney but also on the other islands. The total population in winter is regularly 5-6,000 with the population centred on the Walney/Foulney area, feeding mainly on the Rampside mussel beds. Despite this abundance on the west of the Bay it is surprisingly rare elsewhere with only occasional flocks reaching the Heysham area and the Wyre.

LONG-TAILED DUCK

A regular but uncommon winter visitor, usually 2 or 3 sightings each winter, with most records from South Walney and the Morecambe area, occasional on the island waters. Most records are of female or immature birds.

COMMON SCOTER
The drake is all black except for an orange bill; the duck is dark with a pale cheek patch.

This diving duck is usually restricted to the mouth of the Bay and therefore is difficult to count with flocks sitting well offshore. Flocks of up to 1,500 have been reported off South Walney and Foulney, but this is probably exceptional and the wintering population in that area is probably around the 500 mark. Occasional records from elsewhere in the Bay are usually of single birds or small groups often after gales. Peak numbers appear in early spring and late autumn.

VELVET SCOTER
An irregular winter visitor, usually single birds, with most records from South Walney and off Morecambe.

GOLDENEYE
The drake has a dark head, with a prominent white spot near the bill, and a striking white and black body. Females and immatures have brown heads with no spot and a distinctive white neck ring, and large square wing patches.

Well-distributed throughout the Bay, the largest numbers are usually in the lower reaches. Up to 50 winter off Walney with similar numbers off Foulney. Up to 70 have been recorded in the Leven estuary. Largest numbers occur off Morecambe with recent counts of up to 200 birds. Up to 100 frequent the Lune estuary. Inland Cavendish Dock holds up to 50 and Leighton Moss 20. Females and immatures predominate, especially inland. First arrivals are usually noted in early October, most have left by April but a few linger in some years into May.

SMEW
An uncommon winter visitor. One or two most years between November and March, usually on the inland waters, but on the estuaries during cold spells. During very severe winters there is often an influx and up to 10 have been recorded.

RED-BREASTED MERGANSER
The drake has a distinctive green head and crest, pale chestnut body and grey flanks, the female has a generally grey body and a crested brown head. The bill is the typical long bill of the 'sawbills'. Breeds in small numbers in the Walney area and by the Leven and Kent estuaries.

Small numbers can be seen anywhere in the Bay throughout the year. Winter birds are almost exclusively marine, except for Cavendish Dock where up to 250 have been recorded. The largest flocks occur off Morecambe with a peak population of about 500 birds. Up to 50 occur off South Walney, Foulney and the Kent, Leven and Lune estuaries.

GOOSANDER

The male has pinkish white breast and underparts a black back and glossy green head. The female is very similar to the red-breasted merganser but can be distinguished by the sharp division between the chestnut neck and white chest.

Now well established as a breeding bird on the Lune, Kent and Leven river systems. Only occurs in small numbers on the estuaries especially from November to March. The upper Kent and Leven hold up to 15 and small numbers occur off Morecambe. Inland there are up to 10 irregularly at Leighton Moss and the Allen Pool.

RUDDY DUCK

This escape from captivity has become well-established in several parts of Britain, with a good population as close to the area as South Lancashire and Cheshire. To the Bay it is only an occasional wanderer with most records from Leighton Moss.

CHAPTER 3
Gulls, Terns, Seabirds and Other Species Occuring On the Coast.

The gull population of Morecambe Bay is extremely large right throughout the year. The intertidal areas are feeding grounds for some species, they roost at high tide on the salt marshes, shingle beaches and fields. Many other gulls use the sandbanks of the Bay as a night-time roost, after feeding inland during the day, mainly on fields or rubbish tips. These birds simply float on the water during a night-time tide.

All the terns are strictly summer visitors and are present either as breeding birds or passage migrants.

The mouth of the Bay is the best area to watch for seabirds as many cross the Bay at this point. South Walney and Rossall Point are the best watching sites. Seabirds only occur further up the Bay when driven to seek shelter during gales; on occasions some are blown inland.

GULLS
MEDITERRANEAN GULL
A rare but increasing visitor, not recorded until 1976. There have been c. 10 records since then mainly in late summer.

LITTLE GULL
A scarce but increasing passage migrant. Singles or small groups mainly of immature birds occur in the period April to June. There is a smaller autumn passage, and recently there have been several winter records.

BLACK-HEADED GULL
Smallest of the commoner gulls, this well-known species has a conspicuous chocolate-brown head in summer plumage. In winter the 'hood' is absent except for a dark spot behind the eye. The legs and bill are red.

Lesser black-backed gull - Walney

There are two major breeding colonies; Foulney Island and Leighton Moss/Allen Pool. Both have around 7-800 pairs. Numbers arrive at the colonies in early March and stay until early July.

Very common throughout the year on the low-lying fields and at times on the intertidal area. Very large numbers use the sandbanks as a roost site after feeding inland during the day. Such major roosts can at times (especially in winter) hold thousands and at times tens of thousands of birds including many common gulls. The largest roosts are located on the upper Kent and Leven estuaries, off Hest Bank and near Knott End.

COMMON GULL

Rather like a small edition of the herring gull, but the mantle is pale grey, pink legs and greenish-yellow bill.

This species is mainly a winter visitor although small numbers of immature birds can be seen in summer often around the black-headed gull colonies. A marked influx of adults take place in late July. At this time some numbers can be seen on the salt marshes and intertidal areas. In winter the bulk of the population feeds inland, flying back to roost on the sandbanks as described for black-headed gulls. A passage of common gulls is evident in March when many immature birds appear and numbers of adults decline, leaving very few by mid-April.

LESSER BLACK-BACKED GULL

This gull has slate grey upper-parts contrasting with the dark wing tips; legs and bill yellow with a marked red spot.

The breeding population on Walney is extremely large. In the early 1970's it was estimated at c. 25,000 pairs but there has been a gradual decline to c. 17-18,000 pairs. This gull became established in small numbers at Walney in the 1920's and 30's at which time large numbers of black-headed gulls and terns also nested. The growth of the colony was slow at first but gathered momentum in the 1950's climbing from 520 pairs in 1950 to 12,000 pairs seven years later. Increase continued in the 1960's and the total population of this species and the herring gull was 19,000 in 1965 and c. 50,000 in 1972. Only a few pairs of black-headed gulls now nest at Walney and terns only breed occasionally.

The bulk of the lesser black-backed gull population is migratory, most moving to Iberia for the winter. Wintering numbers have increased in recent years and upwards of 1,000 may now winter, the bulk centred on Morecambe. New arrivals are evident in late February with a large influx in March and early April. There is a return movement from August to October.

HERRING GULL

This species is similar to the lesser black-backed gull but the mantle is pale grey. Pink legs and a yellow bill with a red spot are other points of recognition.

The breeding population at South Walney peaked in the 1970's at c. 25,000 pairs but has declined somewhat since then, the build-up of the population at Walney is described under the previous species.

This is the commonest gull on the intertidal area, even in winter large numbers frequent the Walney area and scavenge on the local rubbish tips. Tips at Lancaster and Carnforth are also well patronised. The night time roosts are located on the sandbanks as described under black-headed gull.

ICELAND GULL

A scarce winter visitor. Single birds recorded irregularly, mainly immatures from December to April, usually on the rubbish tips.

GLAUCOUS GULL

A regular winter visitor in very small numbers, usually single birds both adult and immatures but more often the later. Many records are from the rubbish tips, especially Walney and Lancaster.

Sandwich tern - Foulney

GREAT BLACK-BACKED GULL

This is the largest of the gulls, has black upper-parts, white body and head, pink legs and a yellow bill with a prominent red spot.

Up to 20 pairs nest on Walney, and a few non-breeding birds remain within the Bay during the summer. Numbers arrive from late July on and winter in many parts of the Bay with the largest numbers around Walney, Fleetwood and the rubbish tips near Carnforth and Lancaster. Flocks at these sites usually range between 100-150. Smaller groups occur throughout the Bay. The largest numbers occur on the salt marshes from July to September and March and April suggesting passage at these times.

KITTIWAKE

The adult kittiwake is similar in appearance to the common gull, but has black legs, a yellow bill and in flight is distinguished by black tips to the wings.

Except for the occasional storm-driven birds or small group, this species occurs only at the mouth of the Bay. Numbers are recorded annually from Walney, Heysham and Rossall Point. Largest numbers occur during strong winds in September to November and March to May. At times 200 to 300 have been recorded at the above sites.

SANDWICH TERN
The largest of the common terns, the sandwich tern has a short forked tail, black cap and legs and a black bill with a yellow tip.

There is a thriving colony at Foulney which has increased in recent years to perhaps 1,000 pairs, nesting on the sanctuary spit with the black-headed gulls and other terns. First arrivals are usually seen in late March but the main influx takes place in April and early May. Most of the breeding birds feed around the Foulney/Walney area and there is a marked autumn passage in this area and across the mouth of the Bay, with concentrations at high tide at this time off Knott End. Further up the Bay and inland it is a rather scarce visitor with most records during passage periods.

ROSEATE TERN
Usually one or two birds recorded each year mainly with the other terns in the Walney/Foulney area.

COMMON TERN
This species is best told from other terns by its red bill with a black tip. The black cap and forked tail are typical of the smaller terns.

A summer visitor, it has two regular colonies on the Bay with up to 200 pairs on the Lune marshes and 100-150 pairs on Foulney, and occasionally South Walney.

First arrivals are usually mid-April with the major spring passage in May when they may be seen anywhere along the coast or at times over inland waters. Often a large return passage in August and September with largest numbers at the mouth of the Bay. A few birds linger into October.

ARCTIC TERN
Very similar to the common tern but with a completely red bill, longer tail streamers and shorter legs.

A few pairs with the common terns on the Lune marshes and 50-80 pairs in recent years on Foulney. The passage and movements are similar to common tern with which it often associates. Less regular inland and in the upper Bay than the common tern.

Arctic tern - Foulney

LITTLE TERN
The smallest of the sea terns, this species has a black cap but a marked white forehead. The bill is black tipped with yellow and the legs are yellow.

Perhaps 20 pairs breed in most years on Foulney or South Walney. First arrivals are in late April and into May. Largest numbers occur on autumn passage from July to September, at which time family parties or small flocks can appear anywhere in the Bay, but the mouth of the Bay especially the Walney/Foulney area and off Knott End and Rossall are favoured.

BLACK TERN
This marsh tern has all blackish-grey breeding plumage. Much greyer in winter plumage but a white forehead black cap and black mark on the side of the neck.

Occurs in both spring (late April to early June) and autumn (July to early October). Largest numbers occur in May during periods of south easterly winds. The autumn passage though regular is usually just a few birds. Small numbers occur during passage periods on the estuaries, the largest numbers are recorded over the inland waters with a peak count of 70 at Leighton Moss where more usual spring numbers are around 10 birds. Most of the autumn records are from the tidal areas.

WHITE WINGED BLACK TERN
A rare vagrant with six records in late summer, and one in spring.

ARCTIC SKUA
A scarce and irregular autumn passage visitor to the Bay. Usually recorded during strong onshore winds during the period August to October. Most records are from Walney and the Morecambe area.

GREAT SKUA
A very scarce and irregular visitor to the bay. Single birds have been recorded usually from August to December, most often at South Walney but occasional records from the head of the Bay and inland, especially during strong onshore winds.

GUILLEMOT
Black above and white below, distinguished from the razorbill by its long pointed bill.

Regular but erratic, mainly in the mouth of the Bay and recorded throughout the year with a peak of sightings during the period May to June. Walney and Heysham are the favoured localities.

Records from the upper Bay or island are usually of storm driven or oiled birds.

RAZORBILL
Separated from the guillemot by its shorter thick neck and thicker bill which has a conspicuous white line.

Much scarcer than the guillemot, recorded only regularly in small numbers from Walney, with records there throughout the year. Otherwise a storm driven or oiled vagrant.

BLACK GUILLEMOT
Only records are from the Walney/Foulney area, where rcorded irregularly in small numbers.

LITTLE AUK
A storm driven vagrant with occasional 'wrecks' producing a small spate of records, usually from the mouth of the Bay.

PUFFIN
Usually a storm driven vagrant, although is now recorded almost annually each winter at South Walney.

FULMAR
Rather gull-like in appearance but thick neck and bill, narrow wings and lack of black wing tips separate this bird.

Regular in small numbers from March to November at the mouth of the Bay and especially at South Walney. Rare in winter. Occasional storm driven records from the head of the Bay and inland.

SOOTY SHEARWATER
Very rare but almost annual vagrant offshore at Walney.

MANX SHEARWATER
Contrasting pattern of black underparts and white underparts, with typical shearwater bill and flight.

A regular spring and autumn passage migrant off the mouth of the Bay. Most records are from South Walney and occur during strong on shore winds from July to September. Occasional storm-driven birds at the head of the Bay and inland.

STORM PETREL
A rare vagrant not recorded annually but most records are from South Walney during strong on-shore winds in October.

LEACH'S PETREL
A storm driven irregular visitor, mainly occuring during severe or persistent gales during September and October. When such 'wrecks' occur up to 90 have been reported, mainly from the Heysham/Morecambe area. Very occasional records inland during such periods.

GANNET
A large white seabird with extensive black tips to its long, narrow wings.

A regular passage migrant at the mouth of the Bay, most numerous when driven close to shore by onshore gales. During such periods up to 350 have been recorded off South Walney. Occasional records usually of single birds at the head of the Bay or inland.

DIVERS, GREBES AND CORMORANTS

RED-THROATED DIVER
Divers are longer bodied and thicker-necked than grebes, this species usually only occurs in the area in winter plumage, which is grey back speckled with white, white face and underparts and a slender up-tilted bill.

This is the most regular diver, usually present from late September to April. Mainly offshore and at the mouth of the Bay with the bulk of the records coming from South Walney. There is a peak count there of 35, but under 10 is more usual. Occasional records at the head of the Bay and on inland waters, and tide-line corpses are reported each winter.

BLACK-THROATED DIVER
An irregular winter visitor in small numbers, most records from South Walney and Foulney. Very occasional records inland.

GREAT-NORTHERN DIVER
A very rare vagrant with occasional records from Walney of singles or small groups usually in late winter or early spring. Very few records from elsewhere.

LITTLE GREBE
The smallest grebe. In summer it is dark above with chestnut cheeks and throat, pale below.

Occasional breeding records from Leighton Moss and other inland waters. Autumn and winter concentrations occur in the gravel pits at South Walney and at Cavendish Dock where up to 40 have been recorded. Smaller numbers at other inland waters and occasionally on the estuaries especially during cold spells.

GREAT CRESTED GREBE
The largest grebe. In summer plumage it has prominent chestnut and black frills on the side of the head. In winter, grey-brown upper-parts, white under-parts and a neck with a dark crown.

Breeds regularly at Urswick Tarn. Recorded offshore throughout the year with largest numbers in winter during cold spells which force the birds off inland waters. The largest concentrations, sometimes over a hundred at each site, occur off Walney, Foulney and Morecambe.

RED-NECKED GREBE
A scarce and irregular winter visitor. Recorded in small numbers offshore during severe cold spells.

SLAVONIAN GREBE
A winter vagrant, not recorded annually, most records usually of single birds from the mouth of the Bay.

BLACK-NECKED GREBE
A scarce visitor, mainly to inland waters but occasionally offshore.

Usually single birds with records from all seasons.

CORMORANT

A large blackish water bird with white chin and cheeks. Immatures have whitish under-parts. The shag is smaller and lack the white patches. Often stands with its wings held out.

A common winter visitor with immature birds remaining throughout the summer. In winter all areas of the Bay hold cormorants. At high tide they often haul out onto the salt marshes, or perch on the towers off Foulney and Morecambe, or the trees on Chapel Island. The total wintering population must be around 650 birds with the largest numbers in Cavendish Dock where they perch on one of the breakwaters. Up to 50 occur off Jenny Brown's Point. Birds often penetrate to inland waters and up the rivers with up to 30 at Skerton Weir in Lancaster.

SHAG

A scarce winter visitor in very small numbers, probably not annual, occasionally storm driven. Most records from South Walney.

GREY HERON

This well-known species has a long grey and white neck, grey back with white under-parts and long legs.

Two major breeding colonies, the largest at Dallam Tower, Milnthorpe, usually holds 40-60 nests. The one near Rusland is somewhat smaller. Common resident of both wetland habitats and esturine rivers and creeks. The largest populations are at the head of the Bay centred on the two heronries, birds assemble in late winter on the sand banks of the upper Kent and Leven before moving to the nesting sites.

BIRDS OF PREY AND OWLS

HEN HARRIER

Most birds visiting the area are females or immatures which are brown with a marked white rump, or 'ringtail'. The male also has a ringtail but is grey with black wing tips.

Although annual it is a rather rare winter visitor, seen occasionally on the salt marshes and at Leighton Moss where an influx has been recorded during severe weather further east.

SPARROWHAWK

The smaller male has slate grey upper-parts and closely barred red-brown under-parts. The female has brown upper-parts and closely barred grey under-parts.

Well distributed in the coastal strip in woodland, farmland and salt marshes, breeding in woodland but moving to the other habitats to hunt. Regularly hunts at starling roosts, at Leighton Moss up to five have been seen hunting the starlings as they arrive and leave the roost.

BUZZARD
A visitor to the coastal strip from further inland, most records are in winter and often during severe weather inland. Regular at Leighton Moss in small numbers, and in the Grange, Meathop and Leven areas.

OSPREY
A rare visitor mainly in spring but occasionally in late summer to Leighton Moss and very occasionally to the tidal areas.

KESTREL
This bird is well known for its hovering when hunting. The male has a rufous back, blue head and striped under-parts, the female lacks the blue head and is browner.

Breeds in small numbers in the coastal strip. Regular throughout the year over the salt marshes and farmland, with a peak of sightings in summer as young birds move into the area.

MERLIN
The small falcon has dark blue-grey upper-parts in the male, and dark brown upper-parts in the female.

Rather scarce winter visitor and passage migrant, small numbers each winter on the salt marshes or the Walney/Foulney area, often hunting roosting small waders.

PEREGRINE
This crow-sized raptor has a slate coloured, back whitish breast and a black moustache.

Regular in the area throughout the year, with some birds visiting the Bay from nearby breeding haunts. Sightings increase in late summer as young birds move into the area. Occurs in all areas of the Bay, often visiting wader roosts to catch prey and hunting over the salt marshes and coastal strip. Regularly perches on posts but often drops onto the salt marsh.

BARN OWL
A very pale owl, with light under-parts and golden upper-parts, in winter often hunts in the daytime.

Breeds in small and decreasing numbers in the coastal farmland. Can occasionally be seen hunting fields and salt marsh edges in winter.

Most often seen along the Furness coast or in the Pilling area.

LITTLE OWL

This our smallest owl is distinguished by its thickset flat headed appearance. The dark brown upper-parts are barred with white and the under-parts are lighter.

A few pairs breed on the edges of the larger salt marshes and coastal farmland. Seen in favoured localities throughout the year, often active by day as well as night.

SHORT-EARED OWL

This is the most regular daytime hunting owl. It has longer, narrower, wings, pale tawny body and streaked under-parts.

A winter visitor in small numbers to the larger salt marshes and the sand dunes of South Walney. Numbers vary from year to year. Birds start to arrive in September and some remain well into spring. South Walney and the Wyre and Leven salt marshes are the most regular haunts, but in good years can be found in small numbers on most of the larger salt marshes. Easiest to see on the tides which cover the salt marshes and force the birds to the edges or adjoining fields.

SALT MARSH PASSERINES

A small group of passerines, or perching birds, breed on the salt marshes or their fringes and these are decribed below. Several other species may be seen at times feeding on the salt marshes or the intertidal areas; these include flocks of rooks, jackdaws, starlings and finches, such as greenfinch and goldfinch. Their use of the salt marshes is only incidental so they only merit a passing mention.

SKYLARK

This well-known songster has strongly striped plumage, a crest and conspicuous white in outer tail feathers.

A common breeding bird on all the salt marshes and many meadows. Only small numbers winter on the salt marshes, very often feeding along the higher tide lines. The breeding population starts to return in late February.

MEADOW PIPIT

The upper-parts are brown streaked with black, under-parts also streaked but lighter, white outer tail feathers and pink legs.

A common breeding bird on the salt marshes, but never as abundant as the skylark, preferring the upper marsh where there is usually more cover. A very abundant spring and autumn passage migrant,

Bittern, Leighton Moss

Knot, Hest Bank

Left: Water Rail, Leighton Moss

occurring at such times in large flocks on the salt marshes, sand dunes and coastal fields. Large flocks can be seen anywhere on passage but South Walney usually records the largest number, as birds move across the mouth of the Bay. When passage is in full swing it is not unusual to record several thousand birds moving through one location. Most of the movement occurs in the morning with birds often feeding in the afternoon. Most of these passage birds are probably from the upland areas of Britain.

ROCK PIPIT
The darker legs and distinctive call separate this species.

A winter visitor and passage migrant in small numbers. Usually occurs on the larger salt marshes on shingle beaches, when often single birds are recorded, occasionally small parties. Most records are from the passage periods of October to November and February to March.

The continental mountain race, the water pipit, occurs rarely as a winter visitor to Leighton Moss and South Walney.

GREY WAGTAIL
The blue grey upper-parts, yellow breast and long tail are the distinctive field mark of this species.

A passage migrant and winter visitor to the salt marshes and beaches, small numbers winter in all areas of the coastline and inland, but larger numbers pass through in late winter and from July to October.

PIED WAGTAIL
The well-known black and white wagtail with slender legs and a long tail. The continental sub-species, the white wagtail, is easily separated in spring by its grey back and rump.

A common breeding resident along the coastline and inland. Large numbers pass through in spring with largest numbers often in late April and early May; smaller numbers of white wagtails also pass at this time. Return passage is from early July to October. There is also a good wintering population of pied wagtails. Large numbers roost in reed-beds for much of the year. Leighton Moss has a large roost, but small reed-beds can also be used and on occasions they have roosted on factory roofs - for example at Glaxo in Ulverston - and also in green-houses in the Pilling area.

STONECHAT
The male has a distinctive black and white collar, with chestnut under-parts. Female similar but less colourful with brown head.

A few pairs breed in the Walney and Heysham areas and

occasionally elsewhere. Population declines after severe winters. During winter and at passage periods it may appear on the inner parts of the salt marshes or along the edges of the reed-beds at Leighton Moss. Regular on passage at South Walney and Heysham.

WHEATEAR
Both sexes have conspicuous white rumps. The male has a blue-grey back, while the female is buff.

Up to 10 pairs nest on the old slag wall on Carnforth Marsh. A common spring and autumn migrant along the coast. Spring passage can start in late February in a mild year and continues into May at which time the larger Greenland race passes through. Return passage starts in July and continues to October.

LINNET
The linnet is a brown finch with white edgings to the wing and tail feathers. The male in breeding dress has a crimson crown and breast. Numbers breed in the scrub along the coastline especially gorse areas. An abundant coastal passage migrant in spring and especially in autumn from August to early October. During this later period large flocks frequent the salt marshes and tideline. Smaller numbers in winter. Often roosts in numbers in the coastal scrub.

TWITE
Similar to the linnet but has a yellow bill and distinctive call. Only occasional wintering birds. In recent years there has been a marked spring passage, especially on Carnforth Marsh and at Heysham, with up to 100 being recorded from late February to early May.

REED BUNTING
Male has a black head and bib with a white collar. Female is streaked with a black and cream moustachial stripe.

A few pairs breed on the larger salt marshes, especially in the rush clumps on the upper marshes, also on the sand dunes at South Walney. Numbers occur on the ungrazed salt marshes and tidelines during passage and in winter.

KINGFISHER
Although not strictly in this group, this well-known colourful bird is a regular winter resident in the creeks and channels of the salt marshes. Young birds will take up residence at such sites from late summer until early spring. Perhaps there is also a movement to such areas during cold spells.

CHAPTER 4
The Birds Of Leighton Moss

Leighton Moss is situated in a small wooded valley at the north-east tip of the Bay. Originally this area of around 400 acres was part of the inter-tidal area of the Bay, being flooded on the higher spring tides. However, in the early 19th century, first of all an embankment and later the railway were built across the mouth of the valley, excluding the tides and establishing the present freshwater regime. For around eighty years the area was drained and farmed, but in 1917 the pump, needed to keep the area dry was stopped and the area quickly became a shallow lake. Reed and scrub encroached quickly, establishing the natural succession from open water through fen vegetation, willow scrub and eventually mature woodland.

Since 1964 the area has been managed as a nature reserve by the R.S.P.B. The major management aim has been to check the encroachment of reed on the open water and the spread of willow scrub into the reed-beds, and also to try to diversify the habitats as much as possible. Fifty-one acres of the reserve are shallow open water, with an average depth of more than a metre. There are three main meres and several smaller ones have been created since the reserve was established. The reed-beds extend to 200 acres and are the most important feature of the reserve, being the only large reed-beds remaining in the north-west. Around fifty acres of willow scrub fringe the reed-beds with the largest block at the head of the valley. Peripheral habitats include rush dominated grassland, large areas of tussock sedge and a small area of limestone scrub.

Many of the bird species occurring at Leighton Moss have already been covered in previous chapters and their status at Leighton Moss reviewed. This chapter describes in detail the major species occurring *only* at Leighton. For completeness those species already covered are also briefly mentioned.

BREEDING BIRDS
The table shows the average number of pairs of each species breeding

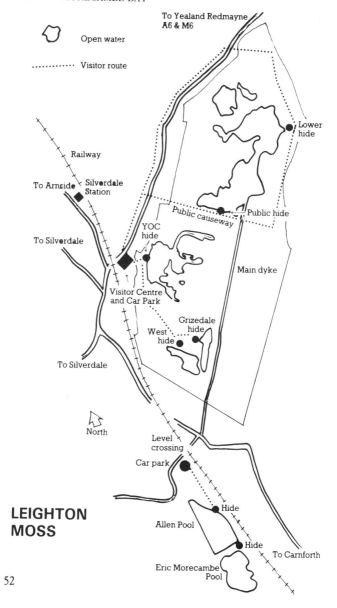

Open water

·········· Visitor route

To Yealand Redmayne
A6 & M6

Lower
hide

Railway

To Arnside
Silverdale
Station

To Silverdale

Public causeway
Public hide

YOC
hide

Main dyke

Visitor Centre
and Car Park

Grizedale
hide

West
hide

To Silverdale

North

Level
crossing

Car park

Hide

Allen Pool

Hide
To Carnforth

Eric Morecambe
Pool

**LEIGHTON
MOSS**

52

Leighton Moss in May

on the reserve for the five years up to 1986. Only the species which occur mainly or exclusively at Leighton Moss are commented on below.

BITTERN

This large, brown, heron-like bird, is richly mottled and barred with black, it has large green legs and a distinctive voice. It is a very rare species with a limited distribution in Britain: there are only *c.* 30 pairs, of which about one third occur at Leighton, the others are mainly in East Anglia. They first colonised Leighton in the late 1940's or early 1950's and gradually increased in numbers, to what is now the largest population in Britain.

Essentially reed-bed birds, they are difficult to see, but from late January to late June the males make one of the most remarkable of all bird sounds - the 'boom'. A loud fog-horn-like sound, this territorial call is delivered throughout the day and night, but especially around dawn and dusk. Under favourable conditions it can be heard over 3 miles away.

Bitterns are resident throughout the year, but are easiest to see from May to July when feeding their young and again during cold spells when they often walk on the ice, or fish the few remaining areas of open water.

Water rail - Leighton Moss

WATER RAIL

This crake has olive brown upper-parts, dark blue under-parts, conspicuously black and white barred flanks and a long red bill.

A common resident which is another difficult bird to observe due to its preference for the dense reed-beds. Its presence is revealed for much of the year by its explosive squealing call. Counts of calling birds suggest a population of *c.* 25 pairs. Although it may be seen feeding at the edge of the reed-bed at any time of year it is easiest to see during severe cold spells, when birds congregate around the few remaining areas of open water and often become quite tame. They are also easier to see during periods of high water level, when they move to the dry edge of the reed-beds and on such occasions it is not unusual to see up to 25 on a walk round the reserve.

Occasionally reported from other wetland areas in the coastal strip, usually in winter. Very rarely it has been recorded frequenting gardens, usually during cold spells.

MOORHEN

This well-known species is black with a white stripe along the flanks, white under tail-coverts, green legs and a yellow tipped red bill.

A common resident, breeding mainly in the vegetation around the meres or in the reed-beds. Occurs in the largest numbers on the meres when the water level is low. During winter and especially in periods of frost, large numbers, sometimes up to 200, feed on the fields at the edge of the reed-beds. Some at least of these birds are probably winter visitors, possibly from the continent.

A few pairs also breed on the larger salt marshes and by a wide range of wetland habitats in the coastal strip.

COOT
A plump slaty-black bird with a conspicuous white frontal shield and bill.

A common resident with a regular breeding population of *c.* 65 pairs. The post-breeding population is usually around 250 birds, but as the water-weeds decline in late summer many move away, probably to Cavendish Dock, where the wintering population is often around the 500 mark, or the gravel pits at Dockacres where up to 250 occur. The wintering population at Leighton is usually around 75 birds. The breeding population returns in late February.

GRASSHOPPER WARBLER
A skulking species, with brown streaked upper-parts and lightly streaked whitish under-parts. It has a distinctive reeling song.

A summer visitor which arrives in late April. Most of the 10 or so pairs occur in the areas dominated by tussock sedge and with some scattered willows. Very difficult to see, except when the males sing from low down in a bush. Most sing on arrival but can continue singing into early August. Most have left by early September.

SEDGE WARBLER
Upper-parts are streaked with a conspicuous white supercilium, the best identification feature. Creamy under-parts.

A summer visitor with a total population of around 100 pairs. This warbler is typical of the dryer edges of the reserve and occurs in the 'interface' where reed gives way to sedge, willow or rush. Most birds leave in August on to late September.

Pairs breed at several other sites in the coastal strip, wherever there is sufficient aquatic cover.

REED WARBLER
Uniform brown and unstreaked above, whitish below.

This summer visitor arrives about the same time as the sedge warbler. It is very abundant at Leighton, the only other breeding colony is at nearby Haweswater, where there are only a few pairs. The Leighton population is at least 250 pairs, but it is a difficult bird to

census accurately, because of the large numbers present and the difficult nature of the habitat. Very much a reed-bed bird with the highest
numbers occurring at the wet edge of the reed-bed where it adjoins the
open water and also in areas with a limited amount of willow scrub.
Most leave in September with a few remaining until early October.

BEARDED TIT

An attractive tit-like bird with tawny upper-parts, long tail and
pinkish-grey under-parts. Males have a blue-grey head and black
'moustaches' which the female lacks.

Very much a reed-bed bird, the main breeding areas of this resident
species are the densest areas of reed. Occurs throughout the year but
observations and ringing shows that a proportion leave the reserve for
other reed-beds in early autumn. This is the best time to see them as
they are very active, especially in the early morning. In autumn they
also feed in flocks on the stone paths, probably picking up fallen reed
seed. The breeding population is usually 30-40 pairs but declines
somewhat after a hard winter. The Causeway, which crosses the
centre of the reserve, is the best place to see this species, especially
from late June to early November when this is the main assembly area,
first of all for groups of young birds and later for gatherings prior to
the irruptive behaviour referred to above.

REED BUNTING

Male has a black head and bib with a white collar. Female is streaked
with a black and cream moustacial stripe.

The large breeding population is distributed right throughout the
reed-bed, rush and willow areas. Very few remain in winter but birds
arrive back in late February and March. Numbers are high after the
breeding season, but birds soon disperse to the salt marshes and
farmland. Breeds in small numbers on the rushy parts of the larger salt
marshes, and also in the sand-dunes at Walney.

WINTER VISITORS AND PASSAGE MIGRANTS

This is a review by bird families of the species which visit Leighton,
and covers both regular visitors and vagrants.

GREBES

These are surprisingly scarce, possibly because the meres are relatively
shallow. The little grebe is regular in autumn with up to 5 daily.
Smaller numbers occur in spring and more rarely at other seasons. A
single pair has bred on occasions. Great crested grebes occur very
occasionally, usually single birds or a pair. Red-necked and black-

necked grebes occur only as very rare vagrants.

SEA BIRDS
Most of these only occur as storm-driven vagrants, usually on gale-force winds with a westerly component. Under such conditions occasional sightings of fulmar, gannet, leach's petrel and great skua have occurred. Cormorants are regular visitors throughout the year, usually single birds, but occasionally up to five.

HERONS
The grey heron is resident throughout the year, the birds coming from the heronry at Dallam, Milnthorpe, there being a regular flight-line between the two sites.

Numbers are largest during summer and early autumn when many young birds appear. The largest numbers of all, up to 40, occur during dry spells when many other areas dry up. At other times the population is usually 10-15 birds. After fishing the meres, birds often sun themselves on the dead trees at the back of the Lower mere.

The purple heron and little egret have occurred as spring vagrants. Both the black and white storks have occurred once. The spoonbill has occurred on eight occasions, mainly in June and July, usually single birds but on two occasions two birds were involved.

SWANS AND GEESE
Numbers of mute swans, especially immatures, attempt to settle throughout the year, but are quickly driven off by the resident pairs. Whooper swans occur each autumn in small numbers, but again are quickly driven away by the resident mutes. Berwick's swan occurs irregularly - most records are in early March as the Irish wintering population move back to the Siberian breeding grounds.

Throughout autumn, winter and early spring the grey-lag flock which winters on Carnforth Marsh, regularly flight over the reserve, sometimes dropping onto the meres. In recent years up to half the wintering population have roosted on the Grisedale and Y.O.C. meres, flighting in at dusk from the feeding grounds. There is some evidence that these birds are the feral population that breeds at Leighton. Pinkfeet pass over, sometimes in large numbers, in autumn, on their way to the wintering grounds further south in Lancashire. The return passage in spring is usually smaller. During periods when snow is lying, flocks regularly appear in the area and consort with the grey-lags. White-fronts, barnacle and snow goose have all occurred as vagrants overflying the Moss. In recent years 2-4 Canada geese have occurred for several weeks in spring, and a pair

AVERAGE MONTHLY DUCK NUMBERS AT LEIGHTON MOSS
1982 - 86

Species	Jul.	Aug.	Sept.	Oct.	Nov.	Dec.	Jan.	Feb.	Mar.	Apr.
Shelduck	8	-	-	-	1	1	2	11	15	45
Wigeon	5	7	52	11	10	7	7	8	4	3
Gadwall	5	6	16	25	23	14	13	10	7	3
Teal	75	325	670	1135	1235	1335	1200	880	670	270
Mallard	1950	1875	1340	850	425	390	335	290	160	150
Pintail	5	90	62	13	3	35	2	8	6	2
Shoveler	60	110	140	165	170	135	105	75	65	55
Pochard	18	10	4	14	33	32	23	60	60	27
Tufted duck	36	16	8	10	7	19	17	30	47	34
Goldeneye	-	-	-	10	13	13	12	13	12	5
Goosander	-	-	-	3	5	3	3	5	2	1

bred in 1987. At other times small numbers occur irregularly.

DUCKS

The monthly averages for the five years from 1982-86 for the regularly occurring species are given in the table. The status of the other less common species is reviewed here.

Gargeney are regular summer visitors in small numbers, occurring mainly from late March to early May. Single males or small groups are usual. Similar numbers often occur in autumn although not every year. This species bred occasionally in the 1960's and 70's but not recently. Scaup and long-tailed duck are irregular winter visitors in small numbers. Red-breasted mergansers occur irregularly in small numbers with records throughout the year. Blue-winged teal, red-crested pochard and ferruginous duck have occurred as rare vagrants. One species that has increased recently is the introduced ruddy duck; this is now well established as a regular breeder in south Lancashire and may one day colonise the Moss. At the moment singles or pairs are being recorded annually.

BIRDS OF PREY

Marsh harriers are regular spring passage migrants, usually from late April to early June. During this period up to five different birds may pass through with an occasional bird stopping for several weeks, sometimes well into the summer. In 1987 a pair nested for the first time. Only occasional records of single birds in the autumn. Hen harriers are irregular winter visitors, usually occurring each year. Most birds only stop a few days, but on occasions one has stopped for several weeks, regularly hunting the reed-beds, and roosting there. During severe cold spells up to 5 birds have roosted in the reed-bed, probably driven from further east by heavy snow. There is one record of Montagu's harrier.

Single goshawks occur irregularly, but its smaller relative the sparrowhawk is the commonest raptor at Leighton. A number of pairs breed in the valley woods and regularly hunt the reserve. Numbers assemble to prey on the flocks of roosting starlings; it is quite a regular sight to see as many as five perched on willows within the reed-bed waiting for supper to be served. They also visit the roost at dawn as the roosting flocks leave. Often the larger females will pursue the starling flocks as they gather, flying quite high in an attempt to single out a bird. The smaller males though, usually wait in ambush until the flocks are dropping into the reed-beds.

Buzzards also breed in the valley and 2-4 occur regularly, with up to

6 birds on occasions in winter. They are usually seen over the wooded hillsides.

Ospreys occur every year, usually in May or June, with a very occasional record in late summer. When present they perch on the dead trees at the back of the Lower mere and fish the meres, usually taking rudd. Most birds merely fish then pass on, but on occasions birds have remained for days or even weeks.

A pair of kestrels breed in the valley and regularly hunt the drier edge of the reserve. Largest numbers are recorded in summer when the young have fledged, but these soon disperse to leave the resident pair. The red-footed falcon has occurred once.

Merlins are irregular winter visitors, usually single birds. At times they hunt the reed-beds and occasionally chase starlings at the roost. Each year usually brings at least one sighting of a hobby, most records are of birds chasing roosting swallows and martins.

Peregrines occur regularly in small numbers throughout the year. Usually single birds but occasionally a pair hunt the valley. At times they roost in the local disused quarries.

RAILS
Spotted crakes, have occurred almost annually in recent years during late summer, they prefer the shallow edges of the smaller meres. Most records are of single birds but on occasions two have been present for up to three weeks.

WADERS
These have been covered in detail in Chapter 2. Briefly though, Leighton mainly attracts the freshwater waders, commonest are snipe, jack snipe, greenshank, spotted redshank, ruff and green, wood and common sandpipers. The shore waders occur only irregularly in small numbers, the small areas of mud and shallow water rarely proving attractive. Snipe are mainly autumn and winter visitors, the other species occur at passage times with autumn being more productive than spring.

GULLS AND TERNS
Again these have been well covered in Chapter 3. The black-headed gull is the commonest gull throughout the year, in winter up to 350 feed on the valley fields and visit the meres to drink and bathe, with them there is often up to 100 or so common gulls. Lesser black-backed herring and greater black-backed gulls are regular throughout the year in small numbers. Little gulls are regular spring passage birds usually in May and June. Immature birds predominate; they appear to

be attracted by the black-headed gullery. Glaucous gull and kittiwake are vagrants. Common terns have bred on one occasion and are regular in small numbers in spring and late summer. Little, sandwich and arctic terns are very occasional visitors, while roseate terns have occurred once.

South easterly winds from late April to early June usually bring a passage of black terns, they arrive with such winds around mid-day, and hawk over the meres until evening. Most arrivals are usually under ten birds but occasionally up to 30 have been recorded. Autumn passage usually produces only single birds, which on occasions have lingered well into October. White-winged black terns have occurred twice.

PIGEONS AND DOVES
The stock dove is an irregular visitor in small numbers. Turtle doves are another May vagrant, most records occurring during periods of south-easterly winds.

OWLS
The barn owl is now only a rare winter vagrant whereas 15 years ago it was a regular sight, hunting the reed edge each winter. Long-eared owls are rare winter visitors too but when they have occurred they have usually remained for several months, roosting in the willows. Short-eared owls are regular winter visitors in small numbers, preferring the rush-dominated grassland, but at times hunting the reed-beds.

NIGHTJARS AND SWIFTS
Swifts are common summer visitors. Up to 100 regularly hawk insects over the meres and reed-beds, increasing to several hundred during periods of cold or unsettled weather. There is only one record of a nightjar.

KINGFISHERS AND WOODPECKERS
July usually sees the first arrival of kingfishers, probably young birds moving from the natal area. If the local population is high they will be recorded right through until early spring, if the population is low they are only recorded in late summer.

All three species of woodpeckers move into the willow scrub after the breeding season, often in family parties. The lesser spotted is much rarer than the other two which are usually recorded daily for much of the year.

SONG BIRDS

Reed-beds are a favoured habitat for roosting birds, especially those which roost communally. At Leighton, starlings are the most abundant and for much of the year tens of thousands assemble on the fields or electric wires before eventually dropping into the reed-beds. This evening spectacular is further heightened by the appearance of sparrowhawks or other birds of prey, which pursue the starlings as they enter the reeds. The largest numbers of starlings usually occur from late summer to early winter and they eventually damage the reeds in the areas they roost. Numbers decline in winter and they may even abandon the roost completely during spells of very cold weather, usually moving to the warmer environs of Lancaster or Morecambe.

Large numbers of swallows and sand martins gather over the open water, then flighting high across the valley before dropping into the reeds. Numbers roost in spring before they disperse to their breeding sites, but the largest numbers occur from late July to early October. Sand martins reach a peak in August while swallows peak in late September or early October. Numbers are usually in the region 1-5,000 but occasionally during favourable migration weather tens of thousands gather. House martins and swifts regularly feed over the open water or reed-beds but do not roost in the reed-beds.

Pied wagtails roost throughout the year except from mid-May to late June, winter numbers are around 100-150 but increase in early spring to 300-500, with them are smaller numbers of white and yellow wagtails. Numbers vary in late summer but in some years 2-3,000 have been recorded.

Early autumn sees the arrival of large numbers of redwings and fieldfares. They join the resident blackbirds, song and mistle thrushes in feeding on the valley's abundant supply of yew berries and later hawthorn berries. Many hundreds roost in the willows and although numbers drop as the berry crop is exhausted, a few hundred continue to roost until early spring. Numbers often increase during cold spells, especially when snow to the east forces them to the milder west. Winter also brings flocks of chaffinch, greenfinch and yellowhammer along with a few brambling - the latter often increase when there is cold weather. At the same time flocks of redpolls and siskins frequent the fringing alders, while hawfinch and crossbill are irregular visitors. Mixed flocks of tits, goldcrests and treecreepers haunt the willows. In some winters large flocks of blue tits move into the reed-beds, feeding on the insects overwintering in the reed stems. Grey wagtails are regular winter visitors and stonechats have occasionally wintered.

Mixed flocks of rooks and jackdaws often flight over the reserve, the jackdaws coming from nearby Trowbarrow Quarry, where around 75 pairs breed. Magpies and jays are regular visitors, the former often roosting in numbers in the willows.

Spring migrants start to arrive in late March. Wheatears are often the first to arrive, feeding in the fields surrounding the Moss, usually with flocks of migrant meadow pipits. Chiffchaffs sing from the willows and sand martins hawk over the mere. April sees the arrival of most of the breeding migrants and also small numbers of passage migrants such as redstart, whinchat, wood warbler and pied fly-catcher, pausing briefly enroute to their breeding grounds. By late July returning birds of the same species start to arrive, some lingering for several days. This passage and the departure of the breeding summer residents continues until mid-October. Unusual species recorded during passage periods include savi's, aquatic and barred warblers, golden oriole, red-backed shrike and wryneck.

The Breeding Birds of Leighton Moss 1982-86.
Average Number of Pairs

Species	No.	Species	No.	Species	No.
Bittern	9	Green woodpecker	1	Spotted flycatcher	2
Mute swan	3	Great spotted woodpecker	2	Goldcrest	2
Grey-lag goose	11	Skylark	1	Bearded tit	30
Mallard	80	Swallow	2	Long-tailed tit	8
Teal	3	Tree pipit	1	Marsh tit	12
Shoveler	14	Meadow pipit	2	Coal tit	3
Pochard	5	Pied wagtail	1	Blue tit	30
Tufted duck	8	Wren	65	Great tit	26
Pheasant	5	Dunnock	25	Treecreeper	6
Moorhen	80	Robin	22	Jay	2
Coot	65	Blackbird	32	Magpie	3
Water rail	25	Song thrush	15	Carrion crow	2
Lapwing	10	Mistle thrush	4	Starling	5
Snipe	2	Grasshopper warbler	10	House sparrow	2
Woodcock	3	Sedge warbler	95	Tree sparrow	1
Redshank	2	Reed warbler	250	Chaffinch	35
Black-headed gull	720	Lesser whitethroat	2	Goldfinch	3
Woodpigeon	8	Whitethroat	5	Linnet	1
Collarded dove	1	Garden warbler	12	Redpoll	5
Cuckoo	1	Blackcap	14	Bullfinch	18
Little owl	1	Chiffchaff	4	Yellowhammer	1
Tawny owl	3	Willow warbler	65	Reed bunting	130

CHAPTER 5
The Food and Feeding Habits of Morecambe Bay Birds

The investigation of the diet of birds is extremely difficult, and only a little is known about some species. However, the most important group occurring in the Bay, the waders, have been studied as part of the Morecambe Bay Biological Study by Tony Prater. This was part of the investigations into the biological effects of the Morecambe Bay Barrage. Waders will thus feature strongly in this account but several other important groups will also be considered.

In terms of biological production an estuary can be up to three times as fertile as the best farmland with nutrients being derived from both sea and rivers. Life is very abundant, although the variety of species is limited.

The major food resource for birds within the esturine system is the littoral animals or invertebrates (animals without backbones living in or on sand or mud). These obtain their food mainly from the water in the form of plankton, which they obtain by siphoning water through their bodies and sieving out the food particles, or by grazing in algae that grow on the sandflats. These invertebrates are present in immense numbers and are readily exploited as a food source by birds. Firstly let's look at the major species occurring within the Bay.

The most widespread and abundant species is probably the baltic tellin (*Macoma baltica*), a bivalve mollusc that is delicate pink in colour. It grows up to *c.* 15mm in length, but most specimens are smaller than this. The average density on the middle shore is 2,000-4,000 per square metre, but in favoured sites densities as high as 56,000 per square metre have been found. Many species feed on this abundant food source. The larger individuals are taken by oystercatchers and bar-tailed godwits, knot and redshank take mainly the medium-sized specimens, while the smaller ones are taken especially by dunlin. The baltic tellin is also taken by lesser-black-backed and herring gulls and incidentally, by flatfish.

Above: Oystercatcher - Jenny Brown's Point
Below: Eider with young, Walney

Above: Coot   *Below:* Lesser black-backed gull

Sanderling, Sunderland Point

Bearded Tit, Leighton Moss

The marine snail (*Hydrobia ulvae*) which is plentiful on many sandbanks, especially those on the middle and upper shores, is very small and dark. When present in numbers the surface of the sand appears granular. Maximum densities reach 10,000 per square metre with an average density of c. 3,000. *Hydrobia* represents a significant part of the diet of dunlin knot, ringed plover and sanderling, and perhaps surprisingly for its size, by shelduck. It is, however not a very nutritious food source, being mainly shell and the necessary intake must be large.

The sandhopper (*Corophium volutator*) which lives in U-shaped burrows in the less exposed shores of the Bay, is up to 8mm long and sandy-grey in colour. Maximum densities are about 9,000 with an average of 6,000 per square metre. Large numbers are taken by dunlin, redshank, ringed plover and sanderling.

Large beds of the common mussel (*Mytilus edulis*) are present, anchored to the stony scars off Rampside, Heysham and Knott End, with smaller beds in other areas. When fully developed, this bivalve is up to 90mm long and has a uniform dark blue colour. Small mussels (or 'spat') settle on the scars during late winter and early spring, normal densities at this time being 100,000 to 200,000, although in places there may be as many as 400,000 per square metre. These densities are drastically reduced by predation.

This abundant food source is exploited by several species. Small spat is taken by large numbers of knot, which feed on this abundant food supply just before they leave on their migrations which will take them to Greenland. Dunlin and turnstone also take the young mussels. The larger mussels are taken by oystercatchers, forming the staple diet of a large proportion of the total population. Mussels also form the most important part of the eider's diet, while especially during cold spells, herring gulls also take them.

Two marine worms occurring commonly on the bay are the lug worm (*Arenicola marina*) and rag worm (*Nereis diversicolor*). Areas marked by lug worm casts are a characteristic feature of the sandflats. Normal densities are between 40 and 100 per square metre, but the rag worm is less widespread and found usually in lower densities. These worms are usually several centimetres below the surface so are only available to the long billed waders, curlew and bar-tailed godwit.

The common cockle (*Cardium edule*) can be extremely abundant in some parts of the Bay, but is often killed off by severe frost and then becomes scarce for several years. Small specimens are taken, mainly by dunlin and knot. Oystercatchers and curlew feed on the larger cockles.

Looking over the Bay from Hampsfell

Only one crab, the shore crab (*Carcinus maenas*) is common in estuaries, where it becomes the prey, when small, of dunlin, knot and turnstone. Curlews frequently take the large specimens.

Invertebrates taken in smaller quantities include a bivalve (*Tellina tenuis*) by knot and bar-tailed godwit. The crustacean (*Bathporeia pilosa*) by dunlin, redshank and knot. The sandhopper (*Gammarus locusta*) lives under stones or tidal wrack and turnstone catch these by turning over the stones or rolling over the tidal wrack. Turnstone also take the barnacle (*Balanus balanoides*).

The invertebrates described are the main food sources for waders. Although they occur in astronomical quantities they are not distributed evenly over the Bay, because each species has a somewhat different requirement. The distribution of waders within the Bay is

therefore closely related to the abundance of the preferred food.

In general, the high level flats, with their relatively high silt content and sheltered position, support a richer fauna both in terms of number and variety of species, than do the lower more exposed parts. The north and east sides of the Bay have a higher population of invertebrates than the more exposed west side.

Invertebrates are only readily available to the waders if they are in the top few centimetres of sand, which is their position as the tide recedes. As the sand drains and dries out many retreat further under the surface into the moist lower levels and so become out of reach of all but the longest billed waders. Optimum feeding conditions, especially for the shorter billed waders, occur just after the tide has receded from an area, or in those areas which are badly drained, so retaining at least a film of surface moisture.

A similar effect is caused by extreme cold weather, when the invertebrates quickly withdraw some distance under the sand and so out of reach. This temporary scarcity of food results in extensive movements of waders from the head to the mouth of the Bay where, especially on neap tides, the sandbanks are less subject to frost because they are covered much longer by the tide. Numbers of birds also leave the area altogether to seek favourable conditions elsewhere, probably mainly in Ireland. They usually return quickly with milder weather.

Waders display a wide variety of feeding methods, some of which are described below. The oystercatcher has two main methods of dealing with large mussels. At low water and when exposed to the air a mussel is tightly closed. The oystercatcher hammers the shellfish repeatedly with the bill until the shell is broken. Sometimes one blow may suffice, but up to 26 blows have been recorded before the shell is broken. The blows are invariably directed to the part of the mussel close to the hinge, which has been shown to be the weakest part of the shell. The other method is used when the mussel is still covered by shallow water and is slightly open. In this case the oystercatcher's hard downward stab with its bill is accompanied by rapid levering and twisting of the bird's neck and head, under which action the mussel quickly capitulates. Close observation on colour ringed birds at Ravenglass, on the Cumbrian coast, indicated that an individual bird used one or other of the two methods, but never both.

Herring gulls open mussels by carrying them to a height and dropping them on stones or hard sand. Some gulls regularly feed on mussels, but many turn to this food source only during cold spells. Eiders dive for mussels when the beds are covered by water, and the mussels are open and feeding. Most feeding occurs on the ebb and flow of the tides when the water is shallower than at high tide.

Smaller waders swallow their prey whole, including the hard shelled bivalves. Indigestible parts are either excreted or coughed up as pellets. The latter habit is widespread among waders and has been used as a method of studying their diet. If one visits a high tide roost after the birds have left many pellets can be found, especially the large ones brought up by oystercatchers and curlews.

Waders feed by pecking at the surface or (more frequently) by probing into sand or mud. The bill is often plunged to its fullest extent. Birds may be seen to make up to five probes in one place and then run a short distance to explore another site. It is not certain if they follow visible clues, such as burrow entrances, or probe at

Wader roost - Hest Bank

random, when locating prey. There is some experimental evidence that this probing is not random, the tip of a wader's bill is extremely sensitive and the sense of touch may be important.

Observations on knot indicate that, on average, a single prey item (often a small baltic tellin), is taken each minute of daylight feeding time. The time available for feeding depends on the tides. During the period of high tide, waders roost, many of them sleeping, standing on one leg, facing the wind, with the bill tucked into the feathers. On a moderate spring tide, some dunlin feed as long as some sand is exposed: they resume feeding when the first areas of sand are uncovered. Roosting is undertaken for no more than an hour. In contrast, oystercatchers stop feeding two and a half to three hours before high tide and the birds roost for a similar period after high tide, which gives only six hours of feeding per tide.

These variations between the species is linked to the distribution of the preferred prey. Dunlin feed extensively on *Hydrobia* and *corophium* which are available on the upper shore as soon as the tide recedes, so they start feeding shortly after high tide. By contrast the mussel and cockle, the main prey of the oystercatcher, is found on lower shores and is not exposed until two or three hours after high tide, so they roost until the beds are uncovered. Knot feed mainly on *Macoma* which only occur on the middle shore and is not exposed until one or

Dunlin, oystercatcher and curlew - Jenny Brown's Point

two hours after high tide, so the birds usually roost for the period in which *Macoma* is not available.

About eight hours of daylight are available in mid-winter. Spring tides occur about midday, so knot often spend up to four hours (two hours each side of high tide) roosting, leaving only four hours of daylight for feeding. This is probably insufficient to maintain a bird in good health, so feeding also takes place during the low water period at night. There is some experimental evidence that night feeding rates are lower than daytime ones and that feeding is also more efficient during moonlight periods. The daily routine is therefore based on the tidal cycle rather than that of day and night. Periods of rest and sleep are not, however, restricted to the high water period, since during low water some of the population will often be resting, usually on a dry sandbank or mussel bed, grouped together in a tight bunch. There is a constant interchange between the feeding and resting flock.

Many species of duck obtain only a small proportion of their food from the intertidal area, their main feeding grounds being the fields and freshwater areas inland. At dawn and dusk they regularly flight between the feeding areas inland and the sandbanks of the Bay. To what extent this is due to persecution is difficult to ascertain. A few species of duck get at least some of their food from the intertidal area. Shelduck is one species, that (except for much of the breeding season) feeds exclusively on the intertidal area. It lives on the marine snail *hydrobia* which they take in great quantities, swishing the bill from side to side either at the edge of the tide or on the wetter areas of sand. Pintail also exploit the same food source, but they also flight inland regularly to stubble and flooded fields. The feeding habitats of the eider taking mussels has already been described. Wigeon graze the short turf of the salt marshes, and if not persecuted they do so during the day especially at high tide.

The arable areas bordering the south bank of the Lune and in a few other areas support the highest populations of wildfowl. Here the large flocks of pinkfeet feed during the day, on stubble or potato fields or - especially later in the winter - on grassland. They flight at dusk to roost on the sandbanks of the Lune. Grey-lag geese graze mainly on the upper-part of Carnforth Marsh, only moving to grassland inland when the salt marsh grass has been exhausted.

Seaducks, cormorants, divers and auks get their food by diving in the deeper areas of the Bay.

A visit to the large gull colony on South Walney, especially when the young are well grown, can give useful clues as to the diet of the birds. The remains of food brought in is often lying round the nest and suggests that pairs specialise in their food searching. Many scavenge on rubbish tips. Others feed on fish offal which they probably get from Fleetwood docks or by following coastal trawlers. Other nests are surrounded by mussel or cockle shells or the remains of crabs, revealing that some specialise in marine creatures from the intertidal areas.

Terns can be watched bringing in food to their chicks, usually sand-eels. The sandwich tern feeds mainly at the mouth of the Bay and out into the Irish sea. Other terns can often be seen fishing in channels and creeks further up the Bay. When a fish is sighted a tern checks in flight, often hovering briefly before plunging head first into the water. One recent new food source is the outflow from the nuclear power station at Heysham. Here the upsurge and rapid movement of the water brings fish to the surface, and gulls, terns and occasionally seabirds have been quick to exploit this.

Turning briefly to the Leighton Moss specialities we find that bitterns are difficult birds to study because they feed mainly in cover,

71

but observations suggest they feed mainly on eels, sticklebacks, frogs, freshwater invertebrates, small mammals and even the eggs and young of other bird species. The bearded tit has been well studied. From spring to early autumn they feed on reed-bed insects, but in late September and on into October they change to reed seeds. Problems occur for this species when deep snow covers the reed seeds in winter but fortunately this is rare in our area.

Further study is needed into the feeding ecology of many species, but the dependence and adaptation to the tidal cycle by all forms of life occurring in an estuary is evident. The inflow of nutrients combined with the sun's warmth provide the right conditions for many life forms to flourish. The astronomical numbers of invertebrates depend on the vast clouds of plankton and, in turn, provide sustenance for the birds. So the shallow waters and sandbanks of Morecambe Bay, regarded by many as desolate or even sterile, in reality support a staggering quantity of life forms, to delight and interest those who have the time and patience to investigate them.

CHAPTER 6
The Migration and Movements
of Morecambe Bay Birds

During a year tens of thousands of birds visit Morecambe Bay. To many of the waders and wildfowl it is a winter home, a refuge from the severe winters which make their Arctic breeding grounds untenable. To others such as the terns and some of the gulls, the Bay is a breeding area which they leave, after raising their young, for milder climates further south. A third group regards the Bay as a staging post or refuelling halt on journeys between the breeding grounds in the Arctic and the wintering ground in southern Europe or Africa. These birds migrate in a series of 'hops', often of several hundred miles, lingering at suitable places en route to rest and feed before continuing.

Seasonal changes in numbers and species of birds in an area are evident to even the casual observer. Much of our knowledge of the destinations and routes used by these migrants has come from attaching numbered rings to the legs of a representative sample. Locally over 18,000 gulls and terns have been ringed as chicks or fledglings. Most waders are marked when full grown. A group of ornithologists who make up the Morecambe Bay Wader Group use mist nests (a method of catching birds in flight, in the case of waders mainly at night) and cannon nets (electrically fired nets which catch birds on the ground). Over 50,000 waders have been ringed by the Group in recent years. A proportion of those caught have already been ringed elsewhere in Britain or abroad. By studying points of recovery of ringed birds, a detailed picture of migration is emerging. The table shows the countries where ringed waders have been reported from and gives a good example of the information that ringing can produce.

Let's take a detailed look at several wader species. Large numbers of dunlin winter within the Bay. Ringing has shown that they breed in Scandinavia and Northern Russia, after which they move along the coast of the Baltic - mainly adults during July and many young birds during August and September. Many birds spend the late summer on the shores of the North Sea, moulting and replacing their feathers before moving across to Morecambe Bay in October. The return migration gets underway in March and is completed much more quickly than the autumn passage, birds taking a similar route. Many birds are back on the breeding grounds by mid-April, although some still linger in the Bay, especially in a late spring, until mid-May. On the other hand, dunlin which breed in north Scotland, Iceland and Greenland do *not* winter in the Bay but pass through in July and August and again in April and May. They winter in southern Europe and Africa, and spend at most only a few weeks each year in the Bay, feeding up and preparing for the next leg of their journey.

Research into the migration of the knot has revealed that the bulk of the birds breed in Greenland with a few in Arctic Canada. Twenty-nine birds have been recovered on or near the breeding grounds in Greenland. The knot make the long journey to the breeding grounds in two stages - from Britain to Iceland, refuelling there before making the next 'hop' to Greenland, flighting right over the Greenland ice-cap to breed on the west coast area and on into Canada. The use of Iceland as a refuelling stop is indicated by the recovery of 85 locally ringed knot in Iceland, all in May or August during the passage period.

Many of the knot found in Iceland were caught as part of a research programme so they were also weighed. From the weights obtained in Iceland and the Bay we can discover what fuel reserves (in the form of fat) are needed to undertake the long sea crossing from Britain to Iceland. In mid-winter a knot weighed on average 150-160 grams, but just before leaving the Bay in late April or early May the average weight increased to 200-210 grams. A bird's weight on arrival in Iceland was about 160 grams. On the average it takes about 40 grams of fuel in the form of fat to enable a knot to fly the 960 miles of a direct crossing to Iceland. Taking an average flying speed to be about 40-50 m.p.h. it would take a bird about 20 hours to fly non-stop from Morecambe Bay to Iceland. Before leaving Iceland, a knot must take on more reserves of fat to allow it to undertake the even longer sea crossing to Greenland. Ringing returns show that the adult knot returns through Iceland in August. Some fly straight to Morecambe Bay, but the majority take a more easterly route than in spring, spending the late summer and autumn on the shores of the North Sea, especially in the Netherlands and the Wash. Here the adults undergo their annual moult before moving across to Morecambe Bay in early winter. The young birds appear to migrate later than their parents, some also move further south, for young birds ringed in the Bay in September and early October have been found wintering in Iberia.

Flock of knot - Hest Bank

Lesser black-backed gulls are mainly migratory, although numbers remaining for the winter have increased recently. This species shows an interesting difference between adult and young birds. The adult birds mainly winter in Spain or Portugal, with very few crossing the Straits of Gibraltar to North Africa. However, large numbers of young birds, especially in their first winter, cross into Africa, some going as far south as Mauritania in West Africa and the Canary Islands. Locally bred terns migrate even further south: there are ringing returns from West Africa, especially Ghana. The young birds again tend to go further south than the adults.

Most of our wintering wildfowl originate in northern Europe (especially duck such as wigeon, teal and goldeneye) or Iceland and Greenland, the breeding grounds of pinkfeet and whooper swan. They move south and west to escape the cold winters. Shelduck by contrast have a migration that takes them east, when most other species are moving west. Almost all the adult shelduck fly to the Heligoland Bight in late June and July. They moult there, becoming flightless for a period. The young, which cannot fly by the time the adults leave, are gathered together into large groups or 'creeches', attended by a few remaining adults. The return migration starts in September, and most adults are back by October. For the rest of the year the shelduck is sedentary.

Ringing has also revealed information about the lifespan of birds. The local record for longevity is a common tern ringed as a nestling on Walney Island in June 1929. The bird was found dead at Ravenglass 25 years later. This record may be soon surpassed by a mute swan, which was ringed at Oxford as a young bird but has bred at Leighton Moss for many years, and at the time of writing is still alive and in its twenty-fifth year. It proved its virility by fathering 8 young in 1986! Lesser black-backed gulls have been known to live for up to 18 years and oystercatcher, knot and dunlin for 12 years. These long-lived birds are the exception. The average life expectancy of most species is much shorter; between one to three years. A very heavy mortality occurs in the first year of life, with the risk of death being highest during the first few inexperienced months after fledging.

Many species associated with the Bay travel immense distances, often crossing hundreds of miles of featureless ocean several times in the course of a lifetime. It is a stimulating yet sobering thought, as one watches a flock of knot in early May, to realise that a few days later the birds will be in Greenland, or a flock of ringed plover busily feeding on the edge of the tide in August will shortly leave for Iberia or North Africa: journeys which they undertake as part of their strategy for survival.

Country	OYSTERCATCHER	RINGED PLOVER	GOLDEN PLOVER	LAPWING	KNOT	SANDERLING	DUNLIN	SNIPE	WOODCOCK	CURLEW	REDSHANK	TURNSTONE
U.S.S.R.	1						4			9		
Finland	32				3		38					2
Norway		1			1		54					
Sweden	4	3			5		92	1	1	1	1	1
Denmark					2		30					
Poland	1	1			8		15			1		
Germany					8	2	23					
Netherlands		4					18					
Belgium							1					
Faeroes	15	1										
Iceland	7	1			85		12				11	2
Greenland					29		2					1
Canada				4								
France		8			7	2	6			1		
Italy					1	1						
Spain				4	1		5					
Portugal		1					4					
Morocco		2				1	11					
Mauritania		1				2	4					1
Ghana						1						

Countries of Recovery of Birds Ringed or Controlled in the Bay

CHAPTER 7
Where To Watch Birds In Morecambe Bay

This is a brief account of good bird watching sites around the Bay. There is public access to all the sites listed but permission to visit any other area must be obtained from the landowner. When visiting any site please take the utmost care not to disturb birds, especially breeding and roosting birds, and also other wildlife and plants.

At coastal sites the best tide height for a visit is given; tide heights are those for Liverpool which are the most readily available. Remember that the tide on the west and north of the Bay is about 15 minutes later than the east and also remember the warning given in the first chapter that the tides can be blown higher than predicted by onshore gales. Always consult the tide-table before setting out. All the sites listed are also shown on the maps, but for greater detail consult the Ordnance Survey maps. Map numbers 96, 97 and 102 in the 1:50,000 series cover the area.

Access details are given for all sites, and while those for reserves are accurate at the time of publication, they may change, so it is advisable to consult the publications of the organisation concerned, mainly the Cumbria Naturalists' Trust and the RSPB.

SOUTH WALNEY NATURE RESERVE
AND BIRD OBSERVATORY

A reserve of the Cumbria Naturalists' Trust. Breeding gulls, eiders, occasional terns. Best site in the Bay for sea bird watching, especially on westerly gales. Winter wildfowl. Wader roost on all tides and low tide feeding area. Four hides, also bird observatory with trapping facilities for passerines.

Access: Open every day but Mondays, (also open Bank Holiday Mondays) 10.00-17.00. Permits on arrival, 50p adults, children 25p. Warden: Tim Dean, South Walney Nature Reserve Coastguard Cottages, South Walney, Barrow-in-Furness, Cumbria. Tel: (0229) 41066.

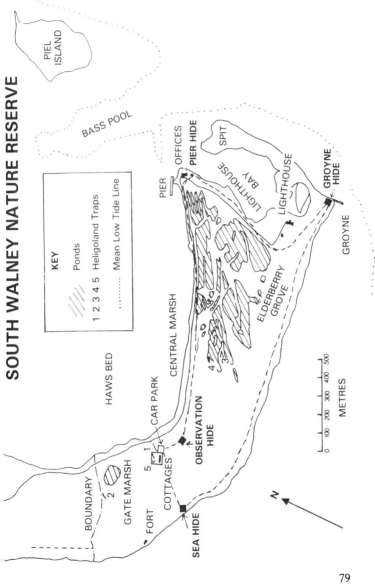

SOUTH WALNEY NATURE RESERVE

KEY

Ponds

1 2 3 4 5 Heligoland Traps

.... Mean Low Tide Line

PIEL ISLAND

BASS POOL

HAWS BED

OFFICES

PIER HIDE

PIER

SPIT

LIGHTHOUSE BAY

LIGHTHOUSE

GROYNE HIDE

GROYNE

CENTRAL MARSH

ELDERBERRY GROVE

CAR PARK

OBSERVATION HIDE

4 3

GATE MARSH

BOUNDARY

2

5

1

COTTAGES

FORT

SEA HIDE

N

METRES

0 100 200 300 400 500

79

After crossing the bridge from Barrow to Walney, turn immediately left along Ocean Road, which shortly swings right. Take the fourth road on the left (Carr Lane) and continue on this road, following the shore line for most of the way for another 5 miles. Car park at the Coastguard Cottages, and permit issuing kiosk. No dogs.

CAVENDISH DOCK

Winter wildfowl, grebes, cormorants and swans.
Access: The road to the Salthouse Mill industrial complex runs along the edge of the dock and gives good views.

FOULNEY ISLAND

Nature Reserve of the Cumbria Naturalists' Trust, wardened during the nesting season. Breeding terns, gulls and eiders. Wader roost on all tides. Wildfowl including sea duck, grebes and seabirds offshore.
Access: No access is permitted to the ternery at the end of the island between 1st May and 15th August. Access to the rest of the island is allowed at all times, but visitors are asked to consult the Warden (caravan on site), and to take great care. No dogs.

Take A5087 to Rampside roundabout and continue along coast towards Roa Island. Halfway along causeway to Roa Island there is a stone causeway to Foulney on the left. This is covered by 8.5m tides and *one must allow at least two hours before high tide when setting out.* Cars must be left in the small car park at the start of the causeway. This may be flooded on very exceptional tides.

ROOSECOTE SANDS

Wader roost on 8-9 metre tides, wildfowl. Passerines including stone-chats.
Access: From Rampside roundabout on A5087 take Roa Island road. Park on road near Concle Inn and take the signposted footpath from the Concle along coast and old railway line.

COAST ROAD, ROA ISLAND TO BARDSEA

Wader roosts at Rampside, Newbiggin, Aldingham and Bardsea, best on 8.5-9.0 metre tides. Offshore wildfowl including scaup at Bardsea.
Access: All areas easily reached or visible from the A5087 except Bardsea roost opposite Chapel Island. To reach this take a track towards the sea, halfway between the Old Mill Cafe and Conishead Priory entrance.

LEVEN ESTUARY ABOVE THE VIADUCT

Wader roost on 8.5-9.7 metre tides, also good wader feeding area at low water, especially in late summer and autumn when freshwater

General view - Walney

waders can be seen. Wildfowl, gull roost.

Access: West side, from A590 to Plumpton Hall. Then walk along the footpath under the railway and along the shore towards Ashes Point. Estuary also visible from picnic area off A590 at Greenodd. East side, from the B5278 down the road to Old Park. Park and take the footpath along the edge of the salt marsh.

SANDGATE MARSH, CARK

Wader roost on 8.5-9.5 metre tides. Large numbers of wildfowl including wigeon, pintail and shelduck, best seen on flowing tide.

Acces: B5277 to Flookburgh, then along the main street of the village to the vantage point on the shore past Sandgate Farm. It is possible to follow the footpath from this point turning left keeping on the upper tideline towards Cowpren Point then along the back of the next locality.

WEST PLAIN MARSH, FLOOKBURGH

Excellent wader roost, but only really watchable on very high 9.5 upward tides. Much movement of waders on really high tides when some go into fields behind the seawall. Wildfowl, short eared owl, passerines along the hedges.

Access: Possible to follow footpath as described for Sandgate Marsh, walking along back of the marsh and coming out by West Plain Farm, then along the road back to Flookburgh. It is, of course, possible to do this route in reverse. Essential to be on the back of the marsh at high tide.

HUMPHREY HEAD, EAST PLAIN OR OUT MARSH

Wader roost on 8.5-10.00 tides. Largest numbers on higher tides, with movement of birds between here and West Plain marsh. Wildfowl, mainly shelduck and pintail. Peregrine and merlin.

Access: B5277 to Flookburgh square, then follow road signs to Humphrey Head. Park at the end of the track and walk away from Humphrey Head along the shore to the point overlooking the salt marsh.

KENTS BANK AND GRANGE-OVER-SANDS SHORE

Good wader feeding area at low water and some roosts on 7-8 metre tides. Gulls and some wildfowl with occasionally large numbers of pintail.

Access: Promenade and path along the shore to Kents Bank.

KENT ESTUARY ABOVE THE VIADUCT

Low water feeding area and wader roost on 8.5 and 9.0 tides. Good wildfowl numbers, occasionally greyling geese, goosander. Herons, gull roost.

Access: Much of the area is visible from Sandside promenade (B5282). Other vantage points are the old railway footpath towards the Bela outflow from Sandside, and the east end of Arnside promenade looking over the railway wall.

ARNSIDE KNOT

National Trust property. Good for woodland and heathland birds. Excellent views over the estuary.

Access: From the Silverdale road turn into Redhills road and follow National Trust signs to the car park. Follow any of the access paths into the woodland and heathland.

SILVERDALE SALT MARSH AND LOWER KENT ESTUARY

Wader roost on 8.5 to 9.0 metre tides. Roost mainly at north end of the marsh and has declined in recent years as the marsh has eroded. Wildfowl and gulls, also woodland birds along the access path.

Access: Footpath from west end Arnside promenade past New Barns to Blackstone Point and on to Far Arnside or do route in reverse.

Jenny Brown's Point

WOODWELL
Good for woodland birds, especially hawfinch, (look in treetops down path to the well) also nuthatch.

Access: From Silverdale village centre follow sign to Lindeth, Gibraltar or Jenny Brown's Point. Park on roadside near Kaye's Nursery or near Wolf House Gallery. Walk down footpath opposite Kaye's.

CARNFORTH SALT MARSH
Wader roost on 8.0.-10.00 metre tides. Good wildfowl numbers including grey lag geese. Breeding wheatears and common waders. Freshwater waders and wildfowl on Allen and Eric Morecambe Pools at rear of marsh. Peregrine, merlin and short-eared owl.

Access: Best vantage point is Jenny Brown's Point, but parking is limited along road from Gibraltar or Wolf House Gallery. Walk along road to Point. Best vantage point is as the road bends to the east. Go through a stile onto the National Trust property; a rocky headland. Telescopes recommended. Footpath at the other end of the marsh is along the north bank of the Keer, past Cotestones Farm and rubbish tip and onto the old slag tips, which provide good vantage points. (Access to Allen and Eric Morecambe Hides is best described from Leighton Moss. Turn left out of the Leighton car park, take next two

lefts, over railway automatic level crossing and then bridge over the
Leighton Dyke to turn almost immediately right down track by
stream, under railway bridge to car park. Then walk through field to
the hides. No access for coaches or high vehicles. No dogs. Hides open
at all times.

LEIGHTON MOSS RSPB RESERVE

Reed-bed birds including bitterns, bearded tits, water rails, wintering
duck and passage waders. Buzzard Sparrowhawk, Woodland and
scrub birds.

Access: On road between Silverdale and Yealand Redmayne. Reserve
Centre is close to Silverdale Railway Station. Tel. No. 0524 701601.
Reserve is open every day but Tuesdays. 9.00 to 21.00 or sunset when
earlier. Members of RSPB and YOC free. Non-members £2, children
and O.A.P's half price. Reserve Centre is open Wednesday,
Thursday, Saturday, Sunday and Bank Holidays 10.00 to 17.00 and
Friday afternoons 13.00 to 17.00. Displays, shop and toilets.

HEST BANK SALT MARSH

Probably the best high tide wader roost on the Bay. Spectacular
numbers, especially in winter and spring. Best on 8.5-9.2 metre tides.
On lower tides birds roost from Teal Bay along to Broadway Hotel.
On higher tides salt marsh is covered and birds flight to Carnforth
Marsh. Wildfowl including wigeon and pintail.

Access: Start watching 2 hours before tide at extreme north end of
Morecambe promenade by Teal Bay restaurant. At high tide the best
watching site is a little further north, oppostite the Hest Bank Level
Crossing. This latter area can be reached by car over the level crossing
with good car parking. The level crossing is opposite the only
pedestrian traffic lights in Hest Bank.

MORECAMBE BAY RSPB RESERVE

Three thousand seven hundred and fifty acres of salt marsh and
intertidal area owned by the RSPB with freehold rights over a further
2400 acres. Full details under Silverdale, Carnforth and Hest Bank
salt marshes as outlined above.

MORECAMBE PROMENADE AND STONE JETTY

Good low water feeding area for waders, particularly opposite the
Broadway Hotel, which is also a good neap tide site. Also off
Sandylands promenade. The stone jetty is an excellent watching site
for, sea duck and sea birds, best on ebbing or flowing tide.

Oystercatcher and redshank - Half Moon Bay

Access: Morecambe promenade is the A5105. Stone Jetty access is behind the Midland Hotel and near the SuperDome

HEYSHAM AREA
Excellent sea watch point, for seabirds and sea duck. Also power station outflow attracts gulls, terns etc. Wader roost on 8.0-9.3 tides on red rocks near Heysham Power Station, overlooked by C.E.G.B. Hide. Ringing Station in area of public conservation tower with migrant passerines.

Access: C.E.G.B. Hide. Key available from Security gate at power station on production of identification. Best sea watching sites are round the harbour roads. Ringing station headquarters are in hut near public observation tower at the power station. Heysham harbour and power station is well signposted on the A5105.

MIDDLETON SALT MARSH
Large wader roost on 8.5-9.8 tides. One of the best roosts for bartailed godwits, knot and grey plover. Sanderling on passage, autumn and spring. Wildfowl, gulls and terns.

Access: From Morecambe follow signs to Middleton. At Middleton turn right at the first junction, which is signposted Middleton Sands.

Continue on this road past Pontin's Holiday Camp to the end of the road at Potts Corner where there is a small car park. Walk along back of the salt marsh toward Sunderland Point, or on lower tides towards Heysham. Do not venture out onto the salt marsh.

SUNDERLAND POINT

Excellent low-water wader feeding area, especially in late summer and autumn and again in spring. Wader roost at the end of the point on low tides, especially sanderling in spring. Terns, good for passerines on walk round and across the point on the public footpath.

Access: Follow road from Overton village through to the hamlet as signposted. Waders visible from the road or from footpath along the shore from the car park at the hamlet. Road and car park are covered by most tides so consult tide tables before setting out and allow time to leave before high tide.

CONDER GREEN and GLASSON DOCK

Excellent low water wader feeding area, especially in late summer and autumn with many waders including ruff, little stint, curlew, sandpiper and greenshank. Wader roost on low tides from Glasson Dock up river. Good for passerines along coastal path from picnic site.

Access: Conder Green is south of Lancaster on the A588. Best parking is at the picnic site by the estuary, reached by taking the road in front of the Stork Inn. Glasson Dock is reached by turning onto the B5290 at Conder Green. Coastal path along old railway from Glasson Dock past Conder Green gives excellent viewing points.

COCKERSANDS POINT

Wader roost on 8.0 to 9.1 metre tides. Terns and gulls in late summer. Some wildfowl. Fields behind sea wall good for golden plover and also corn bunting.

Access: From the A588 follow the sign-posted road which turns off at Thurnham right to its end at the lighthouse. Park by river and walk along footpath towards Cockersands Abbey.

PILLING AND COCKERHAM SALT MARSHES

Large wader roost on 8.5-9.7 metre tides. Large numbers of wildfowl, wigeon, shelduck, merganser and goose roost mainly pinkfeet. Good tern and gull passage in autumn.

Access: A588 runs behind the sea wall. Good vantage point from picnic site, located on seaward side just as the road turns inland towards Pilling. Best observation point on flowing and lower tides is from the Fluke Hall over pass and seawall. In Pilling village take road down side of Golden Ball Hotel towards the shore. Park by overpass and walk on top of seawall towards Knot End. At low tides waders are best seen by walking out from Knott End, onto the sand flats.

PILLING AND COCKERHAM GOOSE FIELDS
Excellent goose watching in winter, especially after the turn of the year, mainly pinkfeet but also whitefront, barnacle and others at times. Birds range over a wide area but with patience can usually be found. Birds flight in evening to roost on Lune sand flats.

Access: Because of wide-ranging nature of the flocks, it is difficult to give access points, but the following localities are usually best; Crimbles Lane area, Eagland Hill, Stake Pool area and Scronkey area. Best to locate these areas on the map and visit each locality, watching for flying birds to give some clue as to their whereabouts.

LOCAL SOCIETIES AND BIRD RECORDERS
The following bird and natural History Societies cover the area; Barrow Naturalist Field Society, (Mr.H.N.Fisher, 165 Greengate Street, Barrow-in-Furness, Cumbria.)
Grange Natural History Society. (Mr.G.Huse, 31 Priory Lane, Grange-over-Sands, Cumbria.)
Lancaster Bird Watching Society,
Fylde Bird Club. (L.G.Blacow, 148, Cunnliffe Rd, Blackpool.)
Bird Recorder for Cumbria: Malcolm Hutchinson, Garden Cottage, Sizergh Castle, Kendal.
Bird Recorder for Lancashire: Maurice Jones, 390 Vicarage Lane, Blackpool.

CHAPTER 8

The Ornithological Importance
of Morecambe Bay

The preceding chapters have shown something of the abundance of birds within the Morecambe Bay area throughout the year. How do these populations compare with those in the rest of Britain and Europe? Ornithological information is improving all the time as more census work and investigations are carried out and published. Bird populations are also changing, many of them in response to changes brought about by man, so any statements made can be quickly out of date. However, this final chapter will attempt to put the breeding, passage and wintering populations using the Bay into the national and international context.

Turning first to breeding birds. The 10 or so pairs of Bitterns breeding at Leighton Moss represent about a third of the British breeding population. This is small in European terms where the total population is c. 2,500-2,700 pairs. Wildfowl breeding populations are not large and only two species are of national importance. The eider is a rare breeding bird in England, the only other area it nests besides the west of the bay is on the Northumberland coast, where somewhat larger numbers than the 950 pairs in the Bay nest. It is, however, a common breeding bird in Scotland and the total British population is estimated at 15-25,000 pairs. The five pairs of pochard nesting at Leighton may not seem large but the total British population is only between 200-400 pairs. Another Leighton speciality that has a limited distribution is the water rail: the British population is estimated at c. 3,000 pairs of which 25 breed at Leighton.

Turning to waders, the total British population of ringed plover is around 6,000 pairs of which 75 pairs breed on the Bay. The total British breeding population of oystercatchers is estimated at c. 30,000 pairs so the 150 or so pairs nesting around the Bay are not significant. Perhaps the greatest spectacle of breeding birds that the Bay has to offer is the 40,000 or so pairs of herring and lesser black-backed gulls nesting at South Walney. This is the largest nesting colony of gulls in Europe. The Walney colony of lesser black-backed gulls is the largest in Britain with 18,000 of the total population of *c.* 50,000. The herring gull is a much commoner gull and the British population is estimated at around 300,000 pairs. Terns are very restricted breeding birds in Britain. Recent years has seen the Foulney colony of sandwich terns rise to around 1,000 pairs - recent estimates of the British population suggest a total of around 14,000 pairs. Common and arctic terns are more widely spread, with British populations in the region of 20,000 plus pairs. The little tern is the rarest of the terns breeding in the Bay with perhaps 20 pairs out of a total British population of 1,800 pairs. The only passerine with a limited distribution elsewhere in Britain is the bearded tit, the Leighton population of up to 40 pairs compares with a total British population of around 500-600 pairs.

Although some of the breeding populations are of national significance it is the large populations of wintering waders and wild-fowl in the By that is of greatest significance in both national and international terms. To be considered of national or international importance an area must hold at least 1% of the total population. The table shows that no fewer than 10 wader species and nine wildfowl species are of national importance and 7 wader species and 4 wildfowl species are of international importance. In terms of the total wader populations, the Bay is the most important estuary for waders in Britain, averaging around 50,000 more waders than any other estuary each winter. In European terms is it probably the third most important estuary. It is of outstanding importance for knot, oystercatcher and bar-tailed godwit. (The figures in the table take account of only the wintering populations but if passage birds are considered, one other species - the sanderling - would be included, with a spring passage peak of 15,000. Four other species would also be upgraded; ringed plover with a spring passage peak of 7,000; redshank have an autumn peak of 12,000 and curlew with up to 14,000 in autumn. Pinkfeet peak in late winter at *c.* 6,000; again higher than the wintering population. In summary then, the Morecambe Bay area is extremely rich ornithologically in breeding birds but its major importance is as a wintering and passage area for waders and wildfowl.

What will the future bring? There have been many schemes over the years to radically change the Bay, ranging from barrages for water storage to crossings for road or railway. These seem to have lost favour in recent years due mainly to the high cost of such schemes. Smaller schemes of pumped water storage lagoons have also been suggested; these would be on the higher sand flats. Another idea in vogue at the time of writing is electricity generation by harnessing tidal power,

Curlew - Jenny Brown's Point

involving the construction of a barrage to regulate tidal flows. All these schemes would bring radical changes to the ecology of the Bay, changing it from an estuarine ecology to a freshwater one, or in the case of a tidal barrage, retaining the marine influence but permanently flooding large areas of sand flats.

Any of these schemes would have a profound effect on the bird populations, depending of course on the scale of the change and where sited. The group most seriously affected would be the waders, which would lose out in *any* of the proposed schemes, due mainly to loss of feeding grounds. Wildfowl may actually benefit to some extent and hopefully the bulk of the breeding birds would be unaffected.

However, there are no concrete schemes being considered at the time of writing. Let us hope that this unique and fascinating area will remain unspoilt with the continual ebb and flow of the tides providing sustenance and sanctuary for its unique wildlife.

**Waterfowl of International and National Importance
Wintering in Morecambe Bay 1969-75**

Species	Highest Average Count	% British	% International
Pink Feet	3000	4.0	4.0
Shelduck	6640	11.1	5.1
Wigeon	4120	2.1	1.0
Teal	950	1.3	
Mallard	4060	1.0	
Pintail	560	2.8	1.1
Eider	630	1.1	
Common Scoter	660	1.9	
Goldeneye	390	3.1	
Merganser	330	4.4	
Oystercatcher	44700	22.3	8.4
Ringed Plover	230	1.0	
Grey Plover	200	2.0	
Knot	80200	26.7	16.0
Dunlin	48700	8.9	4.1
Bar-tailed Godwit	8080	18.0	9.0
Curlew	7700	7.7	3.8
Redshank	6900	6.9	6.3
Turnstone	1670	6.7	Not known

CHECKLIST
BIRDS OF THE MORECAMBE BAY AREA 1965-1987

RED-THROATED DIVER

BLACK-THROATED DIVER

LITTLE GREBE

GREAT CRESTED GREBE

RED-NECKED GREBE

SLAVONIAN GREBE

BLACK-NECKED GREBE

FULMAR

MANX SHEARWATER

CORY'S SHEARWATER

GREAT SHEARWATER

SOOTY SHEARWATER

STORM PETREL

LEACH'S PETREL

GANNET

CORMORANT

SHAG

BITTERN

LITTLE BITTERN

NIGHT HERON

CATTLE EGRET

LITTLE EGRET

HERON

PURPLE HERON

BLACK STORK

WHITE STORK

SPOONBILL

MUTE SWAN

BEWICK'S SWAN

WHOOPER SWAN

BEAN GOOSE

PINKFOOTED GOOSE

WHITE-FRONTED GOOSE

GREYLAG GOOSE

SNOW GOOSE

CANADA GOOSE

BARNACLE GOOSE

BRENT GOOSE

EGYPTIAN GOOSE

RUDDY SHELDUCK

SHELDUCK

WIGEON

GADWALL

TEAL

MALLARD

PINTAIL

GARGENEY

BLUE-WINGED TEAL

SHOVELER

RED-CRESTED POCHARD

POCHARD

FERRUGINOUS DUCK

TUFTED DUCK

SCAUP

EIDER

KING EIDER

LONG-TAILED DUCK

COMMON SCOTER

VELVET SCOTER

GOLDENEYE

SMEW

MERGANSER

GOOSANDER

RUDDY DUCK

MARSH HARRIER

HEN HARRIER

MONTAGU'S HARRIER

GOSHAWK

SPARROWHAWK

BUZZARD

ROUGH-LEGGED BUZZARD

OSPREY

KESTREL

RED-FOOTED FALCON

HOBBY

MERLIN

GYRFALCON

PEREGRINE

RED-LEGGED PARTRIDGE

PARTRIDGE

QUAIL

PHEASANT

WATER RAIL

SPOTTED CRAKE

CORNCRAKE

MOORHEN

COOT

CRANE

OYSTERCATCHER

AVOCET

STONE-CURLEW

COLLARED PRATINCOLE

LITTLE RINGED PLOVER

RINGED PLOVER

DOTTEREL

GOLDEN PLOVER

GREY PLOVER

LAPWING

KNOT

SANDERLING

LITTLE STINT

TEMMINCK'S STINT

WHITE-RUMPED SANDPIPER

BAIRD'S SANDPIPER

PECTORAL SANDPIPER

CURLEW SANDPIPER

PURPLE SANDPIPER

DUNLIN

BUFF-BREASTED SANDPIPER

RUFF

JACK SNIPE

SNIPE

WOODCOCK

BLACK-TAILED GODWIT

BAR-TAILED GODWIT

WHIMBREL

CURLEW

SPOTTED REDSHANK

REDSHANK

MARSH SANDPIPER

GREENSHANK

LESSER YELLOWLEGS

GREEN SANDPIPER

WOOD SANDPIPER

COMMON SANDPIPER

TURNSTONE

WILSON'S PHALAROPE

RED-NECKED PHALAROPE

GREY PHALAROPE

POMARINE SKUA

ARCTIC SKUA

LONG-TAILED SKUA

GREAT SKUA

MEDITERRANEAN GULL

LAUGHING GULL	NIGHTJAR
LITTLE GULL	SWIFT
SABINE'S GULL	KINGFISHER
BLACK-HEADED GULL	BEE-EATER
RING-BILLED GULL	HOOPOE
COMMON GULL	WRYNECK
LESSER BLACK-BACKED GULL	GREEN WOODPECKER
HERRING GULL	GREAT SPOTTED WOODPECKER
ICELAND GULL	LESSER SPOTTED WOODPECKER
GLAUCOUS GULL	SKYLARK
GREAT BLACK-BACKED GULL	SHORE LARK
KITTIWAKE	SAND MARTIN
CASPIAN TERN	SWALLOW
SANDWICH TERN	HOUSE MARTIN
ROSEATE TERN	RICHARD'S PIPIT
COMMON TERN	TAWNY PIPIT
ARCTIC TERN	TREE PIPIT
LITTLE TERN	MEADOW PIPIT
BLACK TERN	RED-THROATED PIPIT
WHITE-WINGED BLACK TERN	ROCK PIPIT
GUILLEMOT	WATER PIPIT
RAZORBILL	YELLOW WAGTAIL
BLACK GUILLEMOT	GREY WAGTAIL
LITTLE AUK	PIED WAGTAIL
PUFFIN	WHITE WAGTAIL
STOCK DOVE	WAXWING
WOODPIGEON	DIPPER
COLLARED DOVE	WREN
TURTLE DOVE	DUNNOCK
CUCKOO	ROBIN
BARN OWL	BLUETHROAT
LITTLE OWL	BLACK REDSTART
TAWNY OWL	REDSTART
LONG-EARED OWL	WHINCHAT
SHORT-EARED OWL	STONECHAT

DESERT WHEATEAR
RING OUZEL
BLACKBIRD
FIELDFARE
SONG THRUSH
REDWING
MISTLE THRUSH
GRASSHOPPER WARBLER
SAVI'S WARBLER
AQUATIC WARBLER
SEDGE WARBLER
PADDYFIELD WARBLER
MARSH WARBLER
REED WARBLER
ICTERINE WARBLER
MELODIOUS WARBLER
BARRED WARBLER
LESSER WHITETHROAT
WHITETHROAT
GARDEN WARBLER
BLACKCAP
PALLAS'S WARBLER
YELLOW-BROWED WARBLER
WOOD WARBLER
CHIFFCHAFF
WILLOW WARBLER
GOLDCREST
FIRECREST
SPOTTED FLYCATCHER
RED-BREASTED FLYCATCHER
BEARDED TIT
LONG-TAILED TIT
MARSH TIT
WILLOW TIT
COAL TIT

BLUE TIT
GREAT TIT
NUTHATCH
TREECREEPER
GOLDEN ORIOLE
RED-BACKED SHRIKE
GREAT GREY SHRIKE
JAY
MAGPIE
CHOUGH
JACKDAW
ROOK
CARRION CROW
RAVEN
STARLING
HOUSE SPARROW
TREE SPARROW
CHAFFINCH
BRAMBLING
GREENFINCH
GOLDFINCH
SISKIN
LINNET
TWITE
REDPOLL
CROSSBILL
BULLFINCH
HAWFINCH
WHITE-THROATED SPARROW
LAPLAND BUNTING
SNOW BUNTING
YELLOWHAMMER
ORTOLAN BUNTING
LITTLE BUNTING
REED BUNTING

Printed by CARNMOR PRINT & DESIGN
LONDON ROAD, PRESTON, LANCASHIRE